Absolutely a la Carte

RECIPES
AND STORIES

FROM A

SOUTHERN BISTRO
AND GIFT SHOP

IN THE MIDST OF
THE MISSISSIPPI
DELTA

We do not claim that all of our recipes are original, but they are our favorites and have been tested and retested and are ready to be shared with you.

A la Carte Alley
111 South Court Street
Cleveland, MS 38732
Phone: (662) 843-6510
Fax: (622) 843-6512
Email: alacarte@capital2.com

photographs by William Powell
artwork by Mary Beth Hawkins

1st printing   1999   5,000 copies

ISBN: 0-9673913-0-X

Printed in the USA by
WIMMER
The Wimmer Companies
Memphis
1-800-548-2537

Dedication

A la Carte Alley never could have made the leap from
dream to reality if it were not for my husband's uncle,

William S. (Bill) Boswell Sr.

He encouraged me and believed in me,
and for that I will be forever grateful. I hope
he is looking down from heaven and smiling.

Thank you, Uncle Bill.

A restaurant is a fantasy---a kind of living fantasy in which diners are the most important members of the cast.

- Warner Le Roy

Table of

Acknowledgments

To my husband David for having a healthy appetite and doing all the taste tests for nine years, for helping me in every aspect of the business, and for being there when I needed someone to talk to.

To my children, Marc, Allie, and Emery, for keeping me young and making sure there is never a dull moment in my life.

To my parents for teaching me values such as doing your part, hard work counts, and honesty is everything, and also for teaching me to eat well and enjoy food.

To my grandmothers with whom this cookbook would have been such fun to share.

To my college journalism professor, Mr. Winfred Moncrief, for encouraging me a long, long time ago to do things in my life that will make happiness possible.

To all of our employees, both past and present, who contributed interesting bits of their personalities to help make A la Carte what it is.

To our cooks, Deborah Hines, Gwen Carter, Lisa Green, and Clara Longmire, for sticking with me through thick and thin.

To all of our wonderful and loyal customers whose encouragement and support helped A la Carte achieve success beyond my dreams.

I thank all of you from the bottom of my heart.

Foreword

What was I thinking? In 1992, I had a home-based gift basket/catering business and was given notice by the city that my home was not a commercially-zoned area; therefore, I had to stop doing business at that location. I loved what I was doing, so I decided to look for a building in downtown Cleveland. I immediately found the perfect building (I was able to see a lot of potential). It had been vacant for several years and was in bad shape, but it had character, and that was important to me. It was built around 1936 and had housed *The Bolivar County News*, which was later the *Cleveland News-Enterprise*, one of Cleveland's first newspapers. Later it was a print shop and office-supply company.

The building was large (4,000 square feet), and it was divided into several rooms and storage spaces. Because I didn't think I would ever need that much space, the size of the building somewhat bothered me. Running a small business in my home was easy, but the idea of running a business in this large building was unnerving.

I called my husband's uncle, Bill Boswell Sr., who was a retired accountant, for advice. He looked at the building and found out the selling price. He then went over all of my bookkeeping and sales records. We both knew that I would need to do something besides gift baskets and catering to make the business profitable. I also had to figure out how I was going to afford such an undertaking: I had to have a commercial kitchen in order to do catering, and that was a huge expense just in itself.

Delta State University had recently conducted a survey that indicated Cleveland needed a restaurant in the downtown area. But I had no idea how to run a restaurant and had no formal training or any restaurant experience. I had never even waited tables in college. Somehow, though, we decided we would have a small restaurant along with the gifts and serve lunch only. VERY SMALL!! My fashion merchandising degree from Mississippi University for Women would help with the buying, selling, and display aspects of the gift shop.

Uncle Bill loaned me the money for the building and co-signed a note at the bank for the renovation and equipment. He told me he would tend to all the bookkeeping and financial matters free of charge in exchange for an office in the building. I was very grateful. I wanted to learn how to run a business, and I told him I would be a willing student. Our budget was not very large considering the amount of renovation that was necessary. We decided to redo half of the building and leave the other half for storage. We had to take it step by step.

Fortunately, David's talent in designing and building enabled us to save a considerable amount of money. At that time he was a cotton farmer, and he juggled his farming duties with the renovation. With the help of a crew, he tore down walls, designed and built the kitchen, pulled up old tile to find original hardwood—he basically remodeled half of the building. We then had the hardwood floors refinished, the plumbing and electricity reworked, and the building repainted.

While all of this was taking place, I was planning what would be sold in the gift shop and what the restaurant would be like. I knew I wanted the restaurant to have a casual, upbeat, and lively atmosphere. I did not want it to be a tearoom; I wanted it to be a place where adults and college students, men and women would feel comfortable. I had no real plan except to serve the foods I liked most: nothing too fancy or too ordinary. After consulting food professionals, I decided we needed to serve really good sandwiches similar to ones served at upscale delis, several types of main dish salads, a homemade soup of the day, and desserts. Our waitstaff would be college students to help maintain the upbeat atmosphere.

The gift shop would be stocked with all sorts of gourmet specialty foods and gift items. Baskets would be everywhere waiting to be filled with goodies. Homemade casseroles were a large part of my business when I was at home, so I wanted glass-front freezers stocked with several varieties for customers to pick up or have delivered to friends.

Our basic business philosophy would be that simplicity, warmth, and humor would prevail on a daily basis. Uncle Bill met with David and me daily to go over budgets and resolve any problems. Our target opening date was October; we had six months to pull it all together. Opening day for the gift shop was October 5, 1992. We chose not to open the restaurant until a few weeks later; we still had a lot left to do.

The original menu had six sandwiches, four salads, and two desserts. I hired a dishwasher and thought I would do the cooking myself. One person worked full-time in the gift shop, and we had three servers who alternated helping the gift shop and waiting on the six tables in the restaurant.

The first day was a nightmare. The customers arrived, the restaurant was full, the takeout phone was ringing, and I panicked. Orders backed up, and I cried. Luckily, our Sysco Food Services representative, Jim Latham, was there that day. He took his jacket off and began making sandwiches. The dishwasher, Deborah Hines, put her arm around my shoulder and told me to find another dishwasher; she would now do the cooking. From then on we were a well-oiled machine. We hired a new dishwasher before the day was over, and Deborah's sister Clara came to help in the kitchen. I worked in the kitchen everyday alongside Deborah for the first year.

We added dining tables in the gift shop three months later, then more menu items. Our largest renovation took place two years ago in 1997, when we remodeled the other half of the building. We now have 20 employees and 52 menu items, and we can seat 100 for lunch.

Our gift shop is still a large part of the business. We have a wide selection of gourmet foods from around the world, unusual decorative pieces for the home, several varieties of whole-bean coffees, serving pieces and accessories for casual entertaining, and a variety of cookbooks. We also have a space devoted to scents. Our customers can choose candles, bath salts, soaps, powders, or bath gels from the top manufacturers in the country. Our newest addition is a custom scent bar where customers can choose a scent and have it blended into lotions or potions just for them.

If only Uncle Bill were here to see it. He passed away at the start of our second year in business. I lost not only my good friend, but also the best business advisor and teacher in the world. I still think of him every day; his massive desk in our office is a subtle reminder of the stern yet compassionate man he was.

Charlotte Walton Skelton
Cleveland, Mississippi
June 1999

1999 A la Carte
CAST OF CHARACTERS

Amber Aguzzi, 3 years, waitstaff (Cleveland, MS)

Joby Blackburn, 6 months, waitstaff (Bristol, FL)

Daisy Bland, 7 years, personal assistant, housekeeping and sales person (Boyle, MS)

Gwen Carter, 5 years, sandwich chef (Cleveland, MS)

Robin Childress, 2 years, gift shop/hostess, retired (Clarksdale, MS)

Fred Cotton, 6 years, dishwasher/maintenance, retired (Cleveland, MS)

Ellanor Ellis, 1 year, gift shop, retired (Greenville, MS)

Bengie Goff, 2 years, waitstaff, retired (Hurley, MS)

Lisa Green, 5 years, assistant sandwich chef (Cleveland, MS)

Mary Beth Hawkins, 3½ years, assistant buyer, sales, graphic artist (Cleveland, MS)

Leslie Hilburn, 4 years, waitstaff, retired (Cleveland, MS)

Deborah Hines, 7 years, head chef (Cleveland, MS)

Jennifer Hunter, 6 months, gift shop (Cleveland, MS)

Henry Jennings, 6 months, dishwasher/maintenance (Cleveland, MS)

Kim Kilpatrick, 2 years, gift shop/hostess (Yazoo City, MS)

Laurie Lizana, 3 years, waitstaff/gift shop (Brandon, MS)

Clara Longmire, 7 years, salad/dessert chef (Cleveland, MS)

Josh Lynch, 6 months, waitstaff (Madison, MS)

Essie Gwin, 6 months, grill chef (Cleveland, MS)

Kristi Pantin, 6 months, hostess (Bryan, TX)

Jena Peacock, 4 years, waitstaff, retired (Cleveland, MS)

Lisa Springer, 2 years, gift shop, retired (Cleveland, MS)

Les Travis, 4½ years, head waiter (Cleveland, MS)

Blake Tyler, 1 year, waitstaff (Cleveland, MS)

Will Weathers, 6 months, waitstaff, retired (Greenville, MS)

Charlotte Skelton, owner, manager, buyer, and "mother to all"

David Skelton, husband, manager, floral designer, "jack of all trades"

CONTRIBUTING CHARACTERS

*While many books have contributing editors,
mine has contributing characters.*

Bill and Aileen Walton, my father and mother
Evelyn Peeples Dudley, grandmother
Alma Bellers Walton, grandmother
Mark Walton, brother
Nancy Dudley, my aunt
Lou Mitchell, David's aunt
Mary and Earl Grochau, sister-in-law and brother-in-law
Helen Skelton, sister-in-law
Mack Skelton, brother-in-law
Dot Kinman, family friend
Rose Miller, family friend
Nettie Kinman, Arkansas neighbor long ago
Mrs. Charlie Morlino, wonderful Leland, MS cook
Mrs. James Shepherd, wonderful Merigold, MS cook
Jan Shepherd, long time friend
Sandy Weathers, friend

Dips, Sauces, Sips
& Starters

Smoked Salmon-Cream Cheese Spread

INGREDIENTS

1	(8-ounce) package cream cheese, softened
4	ounces smoked salmon, chopped
2	teaspoons fresh lemon juice
¼	teaspoon coarsely ground pepper
¼	teaspoon salt
1½	tablespoons chopped green onions
1	tablespoon minced fresh dill

DIRECTIONS

- Process cream cheese in a food processor until creamy.
- Add salmon and next 5 ingredients to cream cheese and pulse until salmon is finely chopped and mixture is blended.
- Chill thoroughly. Serve with cocktail crackers or breads.

Yield: 1¼ cups

This has become my standard party food almost every time I entertain. It is simple to make, and I can vary its appearance. I sometimes make it into a cheese ball and roll it in chopped walnuts. Great taste and easy!

I never worry about diets. The only carrots that interest me are the ones you get in a diamond.

–Mae West

Tex-Mex Chicken on Pita Nachos

Years ago, this was the appetizer I made when I surprised my friend Linda by delivering a Mexican feast, appetizer through dessert, to her door on her birthday! That was back in the days when I tried new recipes all day long! This one has remained a favorite.

INGREDIENTS

2	chicken breasts, cooked and diced
12	ounces cream cheese, softened
2	jalapeño peppers, seeded and minced
3	tablespoons chopped onion
2	garlic cloves, minced
1	teaspoon ground cumin
1	teaspoon chili powder
1½	cups (6 ounces) shredded Monterey Jack cheese
	Salt and pepper to taste
6	pita rounds, cut in half horizontally

DIRECTIONS

- Preheat oven to 375 degrees.
- Beat first 8 ingredients at medium speed with an electric mixer until blended.
- Season mixture with salt and pepper.
- Spread pita halves evenly with chicken mixture and place on baking sheets.
- Bake at 375 degrees for 5 to 7 minutes or until puffy.
- Cut into wedges and serve immediately.

Yields about 100 nachos

Shoot for the moon. Even if you miss it you will land among the stars.

-Les Brown

Three Seasons Cheese Log

INGREDIENTS

1½ cups (6 ounces) shredded sharp cheddar cheese
1 (8-ounce) package cream cheese, softened and divided
2 tablespoons diced green onions
2 tablespoons diced red bell pepper
1 garlic clove, minced
2 teaspoons white wine Worcestershire sauce
½ cup crumbled blue cheese
2 tablespoons milk
⅓ cup diced walnuts

DIRECTIONS

- Beat cheddar cheese and half of cream cheese at medium speed with an electric mixer until blended.

- Add green onions and next 3 ingredients to mixture, beating well. Chill 30 minutes.

- Beat remaining half of cream cheese, blue cheese, and milk at medium speed in a separate bowl.

- Shape cheddar mixture into an 8-inch log; spread blue cheese mixture evenly over top and sides of log.

- Press walnuts on top and sides of log. Chill several hours.

Serves 10 to 12

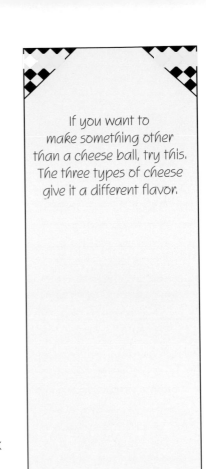

If you want to make something other than a cheese ball, try this. The three types of cheese give it a different flavor.

Open House Brie

We first served this wonderful Brie at the open house celebration when we expanded A la Carte. It is not difficult and always receives raves. When buying Brie, remember that it must be perfectly ripe for the best flavor. It's important to select one that is plump and resilient to the touch.

Acclaimed as one of the world's great cheeses, Brie is characterized by an edible, downy white rind and a cream-colored, buttery soft interior that should ooze when at the peak of ripeness.

INGREDIENTS

1	(1-pound) Brie wheel
1	cup chopped walnuts
½-1	cup firmly packed brown sugar
2	tablespoons Courvoisier cognac

DIRECTIONS

- Preheat oven to 300 degrees.
- Cut out a circle of top Brie rind, leaving a ½-inch border of rind around the top.
- Place Brie on an aluminum foil-lined baking sheet or ovenproof serving dish. Press walnuts into top of cheese.
- Pat brown sugar on top of walnuts and drizzle with cognac.
- Bake at 300 degrees for 8 to 10 minutes or until cheese is soft. Serve with water biscuits.

Serves 12

Age is not important unless you are a cheese.
-Helen Hayes

Southwestern Torta

INGREDIENTS

2   (8-ounce) packages cream cheese, softened

2   cups (8 ounces) shredded sharp cheddar cheese

1   (1¼-ounce) package taco seasoning mix

3   large eggs

1   (16-ounce) container sour cream, divided

1   (4.5-ounce) can chopped green chiles, drained

½   cup diced roasted sweet red peppers

½   cup hot picante sauce

2   (8-ounce) containers frozen guacamole, thawed

     Toppings: chopped tomato, chopped green onions, sliced ripe olives, shredded sharp cheddar cheese

DIRECTIONS

- Beat first 3 ingredients at medium speed with an electric mixer until blended.

- Add eggs to mixture, 1 at a time, beating well after each addition. Stir in 1 cup sour cream; fold in green chiles and red peppers.

- Line the bottom of a 10-inch springform pan with parchment paper and coat the sides with vegetable cooking spray.

- Pour cream cheese mixture into prepared pan. Bake at 350 degrees for 45 minutes or until set.

- Combine remaining 1 cup sour cream and picante sauce; spread evenly over baked torta.

- Bake 5 to 10 more minutes. Let cool in pan on a wire rack. Cover and chill overnight.

- To serve, carefully remove sides of pan. Carefully lift and slide torta onto a serving platter. Cut parchment paper from sides so it doesn't show.

- Spread guacamole over torta. Drain desired toppings on paper towels and sprinkle over torta. Place tortilla chips around torta.

Serves 25 to 30

This was one of the first and most popular appetizers I made when A la Carte first opened. It is great for a large party because it looks beautiful and serves a lot of people.

Fireside Dip

INGREDIENTS

2	pounds hot bulk sausage
1	onion, chopped
3	garlic cloves, crushed
2	teaspoons chili powder
½	teaspoon ground cumin
3	(15-ounce) cans chili without beans
1	(1-pound) processed cheese spread loaf, cut into cubes
8	ounces Monterey Jack cheese, cut into cubes
2-3	jalapeño peppers, seeded and chopped
2	(10-ounce) cans diced tomatoes and green chiles, drained

DIRECTIONS

- Cook first 3 ingredients in a large saucepan over medium heat, stirring often, until sausage crumbles and is no longer pink; drain well.

- Add chili powder and next 6 ingredients to mixture, stirring well. Cook over medium heat, stirring constantly, until cheese is melted.

- Serve dip hot in a chafing dish with home-fried tortilla chips.

Serves 25 to 30

A popular Mexican party dip, this appetizer is good for a crowd on a cold winter night. It is very filling, so serve it with other party foods that aren't as heavy. It makes quite a lot, but the recipe can easily be halved for a smaller gathering.

Don't wear a Speedo bathing suit in public if you've ever said, "Jumbo pizza with everything on it."

-Calvert DeForest

Easy Pesto-Cream Cheese Loaf

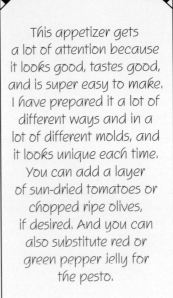

INGREDIENTS

2   (8-ounce) packages cream cheese, softened

1½   cups unsalted butter, softened

2-3 cups pesto sauce

Garnishes: fresh basil leaves, sun-dried tomatoes cut into fan shapes

DIRECTIONS

- Beat cream cheese and butter at medium speed with an electric mixer until blended.

- Line a 9 x 5 x 3-inch loaf pan with a double thickness of cheesecloth that has been moistened with water and wrung dry. Smooth out all wrinkles and let the excess cloth hang over the sides of the pan.

- Spread one-sixth of the cream cheese mixture evenly in the bottom of the prepared pan. Top with one-fifth of the pesto sauce, spreading evenly to cover cream cheese layer.

- Repeat layers with remaining cream cheese mixture and pesto, ending with cream cheese mixture and spreading each layer to cover previous layer.

- Fold ends of cheesecloth over mixture, pressing down slightly with your hands to compact.

- Chill mixture 1 hour and 30 minutes (do not chill any longer or pesto layer will run). Unfold cheesecloth and invert loaf onto a serving dish; gently remove cheesecloth. Cover loaf in plastic wrap and chill up to 5 days.

- Garnish loaf, if desired. Serve with assorted crackers or toasted baguette slices.

Serves 20

This appetizer gets a lot of attention because it looks good, tastes good, and is super easy to make. I have prepared it a lot of different ways and in a lot of different molds, and it looks unique each time. You can add a layer of sun-dried tomatoes or chopped ripe olives, if desired. And you can also substitute red or green pepper jelly for the pesto.

Pesto-Olive Pinwheels

INGREDIENTS

1	(17¼-ounce) package puff pastry sheets
12	ounces cream cheese, softened
1	cup freshly grated Romano cheese
2	green onions, minced
⅓	cup pesto sauce
1½	cups ripe olives, coarsely chopped

DIRECTIONS

- Thaw puff pastry sheets at room temperature.

- Beat first 4 ingredients at medium speed with an electric mixer until blended.

- Roll 1 pastry sheet into a 10 x 6-inch rectangle on a lightly floured surface.

- Spread half of cream cheese mixture over pastry rectangle, covering completely. Sprinkle with half of olives.

- Roll pastry rectangle up, jelly roll fashion, starting at a long side.

- Repeat procedure with remaining pastry sheet, cream cheese mixture, and olives.

- Cut rolls into ¼-inch-thick slices using a sharp knife; place 1½ inches apart on non-stick baking sheets.

- Bake at 375 degrees for 10 to 12 minutes or until lightly browned.

- Serve immediately.

Yields about 100 pinwheels

What you eat standing up doesn't count.

-Beth Barnes

Green Chile Won Ton Cups

INGREDIENTS

4   cups (16 ounces) shredded Monterey Jack cheese with peppers
1   cup sour cream
½   cup ripe olives, chopped
⅔   cup canned chopped green chiles, drained
½   cup minced green onions
1   teaspoon ground cumin
1   teaspoon dried oregano
1   package won ton wrappers
    Peanut oil

DIRECTIONS

- Preheat oven to 350 degrees.

- Combine first 7 ingredients, stirring well.

- Place 1 won ton wrapper in each lightly greased miniature muffin cup. Brush lightly with oil.

- Bake won ton wrappers at 350 degrees for 5 to 8 minutes or until lightly browned.

- Remove won ton cups from muffin pans and place on baking sheets. Fill cups evenly with green chile mixture.

- Bake cups 2 to 4 more minutes or until filling is thoroughly heated.

Yields about 60 cups

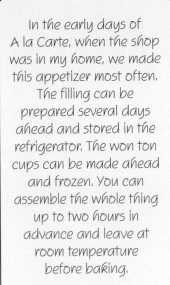

In the early days of A la Carte, when the shop was in my home, we made this appetizer most often. The filling can be prepared several days ahead and stored in the refrigerator. The won ton cups can be made ahead and frozen. You can assemble the whole thing up to two hours in advance and leave at room temperature before baking.

The won ton cups are also good filled with A la Carte Spinach-Artichoke Dip. Oh, this brings back a lot of memories.

Cheese Twists

INGREDIENTS

1   package frozen puff pastry, thawed
1   egg white, lightly beaten
     Salt and garlic powder to taste
¼   teaspoon sweet paprika
2   green onions, finely minced
½   cup finely grated Gruyère cheese
½   cup finely grated sharp cheddar cheese
¼   cup freshly grated Parmesan

DIRECTIONS

- Roll the pastry dough on a lightly floured board into 2 rectangles ¼ inch thick.

- Brush with egg white and sprinkle with salt, garlic powder, paprika, green onions and cheeses. Press this lightly into puff pastry.

- Cut into 1 inch strips. Twist and place on greased cookie sheets.

- Bake at 400 degrees for 15 minutes.

Yields about 70 (these can be frozen)

Mexican Stars

INGREDIENTS

¾   cup refried beans

¼   cup sour cream

1   cup sharp cheddar cheese, grated

2-4 cloves garlic, minced

⅓   cup black olives, chopped

¾   cup tortilla chips, crushed

¼   cup green onions, minced

1   teaspoon cumin

4   tablespoons cilantro, chopped

    Salt and chile powder to taste

1   package won ton wrappers

    Peanut oil

DIRECTIONS

- Combine all ingredients except won ton wrappers and peanut oil. Mix well.

- Place 1 won ton wrapper in each lightly greased miniature muffin cup. Brush lightly with oil.

- Bake won ton wrappers at 350 degrees for 5 to 8 minutes or until lightly browned.

- Remove won tons from muffin cups and place on baking sheets. Fill cups with filling.

- Bake cups 2 to 5 minutes or until filling is heated.

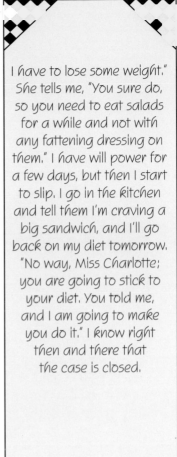

I have to lose some weight." She tells me, "You sure do, so you need to eat salads for a while and not with any fattening dressing on them." I have will power for a few days, but then I start to slip. I go in the kitchen and tell them I'm craving a big sandwich, and I'll go back on my diet tomorrow. "No way, Miss Charlotte; you are going to stick to your diet. You told me, and I am going to make you do it." I know right then and there that the case is closed.

Herbed Pita Crisps

We've served herbed garlic toasts with our chicken salad plates since the very beginning (they are made just like this but using baguettes). I found that these are popular accompaniments to our chilled main dish salads, and they are good served with dips and spreads.

Other variations include sprinkling with taco seasoning mix, poppy seeds, sesame seeds, shredded sharp cheddar cheese, or any mixture of herbs that you like. Watch out; they are addictive!

INGREDIENTS

4	pita rounds
¼	cup unsalted butter, melted, or olive oil
2	teaspoons dried oregano
¼	cup freshly grated Parmesan cheese

DIRECTIONS

- Preheat oven to 325 degrees.

- Split each pita round in half horizontally. Brush the inside of each half with butter.

- Sprinkle pita halves evenly with oregano and Parmesan cheese.

- Cut each round into 8 wedges and place, seasoned side up, in a single layer on a baking sheet.

- Bake at 325 degrees for 10 to 15 minutes or until crisp and golden brown.

Yields about 64 chips

Gulf Coast Shrimp Dip

INGREDIENTS

1	pound boiled and peeled shrimp
1	(8-ounce) package cream cheese, softened
½	cup mayonnaise
¼	cup chili sauce
1	cup minced green onions
½	cup chopped celery
3	tablespoons fresh lemon juice
2	tablespoons chopped fresh parsley
½	teaspoon salt
⅛	teaspoon ground red pepper

DIRECTIONS

- Finely chop shrimp and set aside.
- Combine cream cheese, mayonnaise, and chili sauce in a medium bowl; add green onions and next 5 ingredients, stirring well.
- Stir in shrimp. Chill several hours.

Serves 6

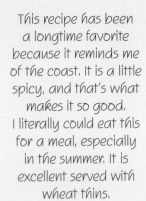

This recipe has been a longtime favorite because it reminds me of the coast. It is a little spicy, and that's what makes it so good. I literally could eat this for a meal, especially in the summer. It is excellent served with wheat thins.

All in all, Mississippi is a lush, pleasant place to live, provided one enjoys the languor of a subtropical climate, kindness, and a relaxed atmosphere.

-Pearl Bailey

Hummus

INGREDIENTS

3   garlic cloves, minced
½   cup fresh lemon juice
1   cup tahini (ground sesame seeds)
1   cup water
6   cups canned chickpeas, rinsed and drained
1½   tablespoons ground cumin
      Salt to taste
3   tablespoons olive oil
      Sweet paprika to taste
      Garnishes: lemon slices, ripe olives, fresh mint sprigs

DIRECTIONS

- Process first 3 ingredients in a food processor until blended.

- Add 1 cup water and chickpeas to mixture and process until smooth. Add cumin and salt.

- Transfer dip to a serving bowl; pour oil over top and lightly swirl with the tip of a knife. Sprinkle with paprika.

- Garnish, if desired. Serve with pita wedges.

Yields 6 cups

I really can't explain my sudden interest in Middle Eastern food. It could be because of the unique little restaurant on Haight-Ashbury in San Francisco where my husband David and I stopped at for a mid-afternoon snack. I ordered hummus, and they served it on warm homemade pita bread triangles. A bowl of marinated lemon slices and different varieties of olives was on the table. Both the atmosphere and the food made me fall in love with the restaurant. This recipe is a jazzed up version of what was served to me. I love the flavors of garlic, lemon, and cumin in it.

A la Carte Spinach-Artichoke Dip

INGREDIENTS

1   cup (4 ounces) shredded mozzarella cheese

1½   cups sour cream

1   tablespoon minced garlic

1-2 tablespoons onion powder

     Salt to taste

     Ground white pepper to taste

1   (14-ounce) can artichoke hearts, drained and chopped

1   (10-ounce) package frozen chopped spinach, thawed and
     well drained

DIRECTIONS

- Combine mozzarella and sour cream in a large bowl; stir in garlic and next 3 ingredients.

- Add spinach and artichoke hearts to mixture, stirring well. Transfer to a baking dish.

- Bake at 375 degrees for 25 to 30 minutes.

- Keep warm in a chafing dish.

Serves 8

This is it-the dip recipe people constantly ask for! This is another recipe that we started out making in small batches and have now increased to large quantities several times a week. It is excellent served with homefried tortilla chips.

(See pg. 166)

A good cook is not necessarily a good woman with an even temper. Some allowances should be made for artistic temperament.

-X. Marcel Boulestin

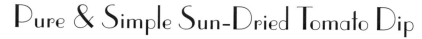

Pure & Simple Sun-Dried Tomato Dip

Why do our wrap sandwiches have such strange names?

As with most everything at A la Carte, there is a story behind these sandwich names. Wraps are different kinds of sandwiches, so we thought they deserved different kinds of names. One summer evening we had several employees over to our home, and with a little help from our children, we created masterpiece wraps. We set up a do-it-yourself wrap bar with flour tortillas, smoked turkey, chopped fried chicken, chopped bacon, cheese, sliced grilled chicken, sliced vegetables, and condiments.

We made a big pitcher of margaritas to help stimulate the adults' creativity, and the children drank virgin daiquiris in fancy glasses. We let each person create his own masterpiece, and this is what we came up with.

(continued)

INGREDIENTS

1	(8-ounce) package cream cheese, room temperature
¼	cup sun-dried tomatoes in oil, drained and chopped
½	cup sour cream
½	cup mayonnaise
10	dashes Tabasco sauce
½	teaspoon salt
½	teaspoon coarse ground pepper
2	green onions, thinly sliced
	Sliced green onions for garnish

DIRECTIONS

- Purée all ingredients except green onions in food processor.
- Add the green onions and pulse twice.
- Garnish with additional sliced green onions.

Yields 2 cups

Great—serve with herbed pita crisps.

White Cheddar and Jalapeño Spread

INGREDIENTS

½   pound white cheddar cheese, shredded, at room temperature

½   cup sour cream

⅛-¼ cup mayonnaise

3   green onions, minced

3   fresh jalapeño peppers, seeded and minced

1   tablespoon lemon juice

½   teaspoon white pepper
    Pinch of salt
    Hot pepper sauce to taste

DIRECTIONS

- Mix all ingredients until smooth.

- Refrigerate at least 2 hours before serving.

- Let come back to room temperature before serving, if desired.

This spread can be used as a sandwich filling, with herbed pita crisps, crackers or vegetables.

The Allie Cat
(my daughter's creation)- creamy Ranch dip spread on a honey wheat tortilla layered with smoked turkey, cheddar cheese, sliced cucumber, and leaf lettuce

The Emery Bomb
(my son's choice)- honey-mustard spread on a flour tortilla layered with chopped fried chicken, bacon, cheddar cheese, leaf lettuce, and dill pickle

The Snoop
(David's selection)- wine-and-cheese sauce spread on a flour tortilla layered with smoked turkey, cheese, bacon, sliced plum tomatoes, and leaf lettuce

Mary's Fiesta
(Mary Beth's fave)- cilantro mayonnaise spread on a flour tortilla layered with grilled chicken, leaf lettuce, chopped tomato, shredded cheese, salsa, and sour cream

Rockin' Robin
(Robin's vegetarian pick)- cucumber dressing spread on a flour tortilla layered with romaine lettuce, sautéed mushrooms, sliced cucumber, sliced plum tomatoes, and sunflower seeds.

Baked Broccoli and Artichoke Dip

This dip is a little different twist on the spinach-artichoke dip we serve in the restaurant. I first made it using spinach, and then decided broccoli would be a nice change. It turned out even better. It is best served warm in a chafing dish or serving dish.

INGREDIENTS

½ cup freshly grated Romano cheese

1 garlic clove, minced

1 (10-ounce) package frozen chopped broccoli, thawed and drained

1 (14-ounce) can artichoke hearts, well drained

1 (8-ounce) container soft garlic-chive cream cheese

2 large eggs

1 cup (4 ounces) shredded mozzarella cheese

Dried crushed red pepper flakes to taste

DIRECTIONS

- Pulse first 5 ingredients in a food processor until blended; add eggs and process until blended.

- Fold mozzarella cheese and red pepper flakes into mixture. Transfer to a baking dish.

- Bake at 375 degrees for 20 to 25 minutes or until thoroughly heated.

- Keep warm in a chafing dish.

Serves 16

A la Carte Fruit Sauce

INGREDIENTS

2   cups sugar

¼   cup all-purpose flour

4   large eggs

1   cup lemon juice

1   cup pineapple juice

1   cup orange juice

DIRECTIONS

- Combine sugar and flour in a saucepan; whisk in eggs.

- Whisk fruit juices into mixture and cook over low heat, stirring often, until thickened. Chill.

Yields about 5 to 6 cups

One of our most requested recipes, this is served as a dipping sauce with fresh fruit.
To be honest, I can't remember who gave me this recipe. And I had no idea it would become such a hit. We now make it in large quantities several times a week, and customers also buy it in pint containers to take home.

Condiments are to food what jewelry and makeup are to clothing. They are not essential . . . but they definitely "dress up" your food and make eating a lot more interesting.

-Kathy Gunst

Skelton Family Shrimp Sauce

It is not certain who started the tradition of this treasured old recipe from David's family, but most agree it was Aunt Lou Mitchell. Every time I boil shrimp, we have to have this absolutely wonderful sauce (it is also a good dip for crackers). I never make it because it is one of David's specialties. He doesn't go by the recipe, and it always turns out great. We've also started using it as a salad dressing.

INGREDIENTS

1	garlic clove, minced
1	cup mayonnaise
¼	cup chili sauce
¼	cup ketchup
1	teaspoon Worcestershire sauce
1	teaspoon pepper
½	cup vegetable oil
2	tablespoons minced onion
1	teaspoon prepared mustard
1	tablespoon vinegar
	Juice of 1 lemon
2	tablespoons water
1-1½	teaspoons prepared horseradish
	Dash of hot sauce
	Dash of paprika

DIRECTIONS

■ Combine all ingredients, stirring well.

Yields 1 quart

In cooking, as in all the arts,
simplicity is the sign of perfection.
—Curnonsky

Jezebel Sauce

INGREDIENTS

1   (18-ounce) jar pineapple preserves

1   (18-ounce) jar apple jelly

1   (5-ounce) jar prepared horseradish

3   tablespoons dry mustard

1   teaspoon pepper

DIRECTIONS

- Cook pineapple preserves and apple jelly in a saucepan over medium-low heat, stirring occasionally, until melted.

- Gradually stir mustard into jelly mixture. Remove from heat and stir in horseradish. Chill.

Yields 4 cups

Frozen Bellinis

INGREDIENTS

1   ounce (2 tablespoons) peach schnapps

1   ounce (2 tablespoons) rum

6   ounces (¾ cup) white wine

6   ounces (¾ cup) champagne

1   cup peach nectar or peach juice (not a blend)

2   teaspoons powdered sugar

¾   cup water

2   cups crushed ice

DIRECTIONS

- Pulse first 7 ingredients in a heavy-duty blender until mixed.

- Add 2 cups crushed ice and process until slushy.

- Pour mixture into a shallow plastic container and freeze 2 to 3 hours, stirring once every hour.

- Serve in chilled champagne flutes.

Serves 4

Our Jezebel dipping sauce for fried okra is also delicious served as a condiment for all meats or used as a dip for the old Southern classic, sausage balls.

Just thinking about this makes me want to spend the afternoon on the beach sipping one . . . don't get me started.

Orange Juice Spritzers

INGREDIENTS

2½   cups sugar

2½   cups water

1   (46-ounce) can pineapple juice

1   (46-ounce) can orange juice

1½   cups lemon juice

1½   quarts ginger ale

Garnish: fresh mint sprigs

DIRECTIONS

- Bring sugar and 2½ cups water to a boil in a saucepan, stirring constantly until sugar dissolves.

- Combine fruit juices in a large container; stir in sugar water.

- Freeze mixture. Remove from freezer several hours before serving (mixture should be slushy).

- Stir ginger ale into mixture and serve immediately in wine glasses. Garnish, if desired.

Yields 5½ quarts

Mary's Bloody Marys

INGREDIENTS

1   quart vegetable juice
1   quart clamato
     Fresh lemon juice
     Lime juice
     Worcestershire sauce
     Several drops hot sauce
     Prepared horseradish (lots)
     Several dashes celery salt
     Several grinds of fresh pepper
     Vodka
     Garnishes: celery stalks or pickled asparagus spears

DIRECTIONS

- Combine vegetable juice and clamato; add desired amounts of lemon juice and next 6 ingredients, stirring well.

- Pour 1 shot of vodka into each glass; fill with Bloody Mary mixture. Garnish, if desired.

Yields 2 quarts

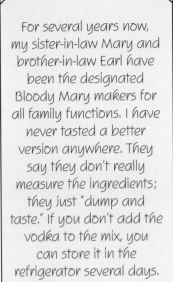

For several years now, my sister-in-law Mary and brother-in-law Earl have been the designated Bloody Mary makers for all family functions. I have never tasted a better version anywhere. They say they don't really measure the ingredients; they just "dump and taste." If you don't add the vodka to the mix, you can store it in the refrigerator several days.

A woman is like a tea bag. You never know how strong she is until she gets in hot water.
                                        -Eleanor Roosevelt

Lemon Drop Martini

INGREDIENTS

1½ ounces vodka

½ ounce Triple Sec

Juice of half a lemon

Ice

Lemon twist

DIRECTIONS

- Combine first 4 ingredients in a martini shaker; shake well.
- Strain into a small martini glass and add lemon twist.

Serves 1

May you have been born on your lucky star
and may that star never lose its twinkle.
—Author unknown

A la Carte Coffee Lingo

espresso [ehs-PREHS-oh]: a very strong brew made with dark-roasted coffee under pressure, served in a tiny espresso cup

café macchiato [ka-fay mah-kee-YAH-toh]: espresso with a dollop of steamed-milk foam, served in an espresso cup

cappuccino [kap-poo-CHEE-noh]: espresso topped with foamy steamed milk, served in a regular-size cup or glass mug

café latte [ka-fay LAH-tay]: espresso with a liberal amount of foamy steamed milk, usually served in a tall glass mug

café mocha [ka-fay MOH-kah]: a café latte with chocolate added

café au lait [ka-fay oh-LAY]: French for "coffee with milk"; equal portions of scalded milk and coffee

café brûlot [ka-fay broo-LOH]: coffee blended with spices, orange and lemon peel, and brandy, then flamed and served in demitasse cups

Irish coffee: a mélange of strong coffee, Irish whiskey, and sugar, usually served in a glass mug with a dollop of whipped cream

Coffee Hints

- The formula for brewing a great cup of coffee is: 6 ounces of water per 2 level tablespoons (or 1 traditional coffee measure) of coffee grounds. Remember that a standard coffee cup holds 6 ounces, whereas a mug holds 10 to 20 ounces. For stronger coffee, use 2 tablespoons coffee for each 4 ounces ($1/2$ cup) water.

- Generally, a blend of two or more types of coffee beans produces a richer, more complex brew than a single-bean coffee.

- Vacuum-packed coffee will stay fresh for many months, but once the coffee is opened (or if it comes in paper bags), transfer it to an airtight glass or ceramic container. The rule of thumb is that once coffee is opened, it stays at peak flavor 7 to 10 days.

- Keep ground coffee fresh by storing it double wrapped in an airtight container, in the freezer.

- Grind your beans correctly. Generally, the finer the grind, the fuller the flavor. Over grind them and the coffee will taste bitter; under grind them and it will be under flavored.

- Coffee tastes best right after it's been brewed. It may be held up to an hour, but after that the aroma will be destroyed by oxidation, and the coffee will taste flat and bitter.

A la Carte Salads

A la Carte Italian Pasta Salad
for a Crowd

INGREDIENTS

2½	pounds bow-tie pasta, cooked
2	(16-ounce) packages cheese-filled tricolor tortellini, cooked
1	cup pesto sauce
2	cups Italian olive salad*
¾-1	cup olive oil
2	tablespoons tarragon vinegar
2	cups walnuts, coarsely chopped
	Freshly grated Parmesan cheese

DIRECTIONS

- Combine hot cooked pastas in a large bowl; add pesto sauce and next 4 ingredients, tossing to coat well.
- Add walnut pieces, tossing. Sprinkle with Parmesan cheese.

Serves 12 to 16

This pesto-inspired pasta salad was developed a few weeks before we opened A la Carte. We started out with an entirely different recipe, and it just evolved (from trial and error and from experimentation) into this. Gwen, our sandwich chef makes this pasta salad almost every day. It is best if you prepare it while your pasta is still warm. There may seem to be too much oil, but the pasta absorbs it after sitting a while. Make sure you sprinkle freshly grated Parmesan cheese on top.

*For olive salad recipe, see page 168.

In matters of principle, stand like a rock; in matters of taste, swim with the current.
-Thomas Jefferson

Baked Potato Salad

INGREDIENTS

10	ounces cream cheese, softened
2	cups sour cream
1½	cups mayonnaise
1½	pounds bacon, cooked and crumbled
⅓	cup chopped green onions
½	cup creamy Italian dressing
	Dash of Worcestershire sauce
1	teaspoon pepper
½	teaspoon salt
1	teaspoon garlic powder
6	large baking potatoes, unpeeled, baked, and cooled

DIRECTIONS

- Combine cream cheese and sour cream in a large bowl, stirring well.

- Add mayonnaise and next 7 ingredients, stirring well.

- Slice potatoes into ½-inch pieces and stir into mayonnaise mixture.

Serves 8 to 10

California-Style Chicken Salad

INGREDIENTS

3	cups chopped cooked chicken breast
2	red bell peppers, thinly sliced
1	pound fresh broccoli, cut into florets
12	bacon slices, cooked and crumbled
	Salt and pepper to taste
½	cup sour cream
½	cup mayonnaise
3	tablespoons Dijon mustard
3	tablespoons raspberry vinegar
¼	cup chopped fresh dill

DIRECTIONS

- Combine chicken and bell pepper in a large bowl.

- Cook broccoli in boiling water 2 to 3 minutes or until crisp-tender. Plunge into ice water to stop the cooking process; drain. Add to chicken mixture.

- Add bacon to chicken mixture and season with salt and pepper to taste.

- Whisk together sour cream and next 4 ingredients; pour over chicken mixture, tossing to coat. Chill thoroughly.

Serves 4 to 6

This is the first unusual chicken salad that we served as a daily special. Seven years ago I don't think anyone in Cleveland served chicken salad this way. I remember one customer asking me, "How in the world did y'all come up with this combination?" It is different, but it sure is good.

Curried Chicken Salad for a Crowd

A wonderful and very popular summer daily special, this salad is easy to make and sparkles with exotic flavor. We serve it on a bed of crisp lettuce, but it is equally good on a croissant or in a wrap sandwich.

INGREDIENTS

3	cups mayonnaise
2	tablespoons fresh lemon juice
2	tablespoons curry powder
12	cups chopped cooked chicken breast
1½	cups diced celery
3	cups seedless green grapes, halved
1½	cups chopped walnuts

DIRECTIONS

- Whisk together first 3 ingredients in a large bowl.
- Add chicken and next 3 ingredients to mayonnaise mixture, tossing to coat. Chill at least 1 hour.

Serves 24

You can put everything, and the more things the better, into a salad, as into conversation; but everything depends on the skill of mixing.
-Charles Dudley Warner

Shrimp-Artichoke Salad

INGREDIENTS

2	(6-ounce) jars marinated artichoke hearts
1	(6.9-ounce) box chicken-flavored rice
1½	cups mayonnaise
½	teaspoon curry powder
1	pound boiled, peeled salad shrimp
3	green onions, chopped
4	celery stalks, diced

DIRECTIONS

- Drain artichoke hearts, reserving half the liquid from 1 jar.

- Prepare rice according to package directions, omitting butter. Let cool and set aside.

- Combine reserved artichoke liquid, mayonnaise, and curry powder in a bowl, stirring well.

- Add shrimp, green onions, and celery to mayonnaise mixture. Add artichoke hearts and rice, stirring to coat. Chill.

Serves 6 to 8

I almost did not include this recipe because a lot of books have versions of it. But this is a book of recipes we use at A la Carte, so I felt I had to include it. It has been a winner since day one. There have been times that we have run out during lunch, made a new batch, and had to serve it without chilling. We then discovered it is just as good warm as it is chilled. We serve it on a bed of lettuce with herbed garlic toasts.

Recipes are traditions, not just random wads of ingredients.

–Anonymous

Chicken Salad with Bacon and Pecans

Crunchy bacon and pecans make this chicken salad truly Southern. It is one of our biggest sellers as a summer daily special. Almonds can be substituted for pecans, if desired.

INGREDIENTS

1	cup mayonnaise
1	cup sour cream
1	teaspoon Cavender's Greek seasoning
2	tablespoons fresh lemon juice
4	cups chopped cooked chicken breast
2	cups chopped celery
½	cup pecan pieces
5-6	bacon slices, cooked and crumbled

DIRECTIONS

- Combine first 4 ingredients in a large bowl.
- Add chicken and next 3 ingredients to mayonnaise mixture, stirring well. Chill several hours.

Serves 8

Cashew-Chicken Salad

INGREDIENTS

8   cups chopped cooked chicken breast

2   cups chopped celery

1   (8-ounce) can sliced water chestnuts, drained

1   (16-ounce) can pineapple tidbits, drained

2   cups mayonnaise

2   tablespoons soy sauce

2   teaspoons curry powder

2   cups whole cashews

DIRECTIONS

■ Combine first 4 ingredients in a large bowl.

■ Combine mayonnaise, soy sauce, and curry powder; add to chicken mixture, stirring well. Chill.

■ Stir cashews into salad just before serving.

Serves 12

Maybe it's the cashews, or maybe it's the curry. I'm not sure, but this is one of my personal favorites. We serve a scoop on a bed of lettuce with one of our other salads and Miniature Parmesan Biscuits.

If you obey all the rules, you miss all the fun.
-Katherine Hepburn

Fresh Apple Salad with Walnuts and Grapes

This is our version of the classic Waldorf salad, and it is one of the best I have ever had. Waldorf salad was created at New York's Waldorf-Astoria Hotel in the 1890s. The original version contained only apple, celery, and mayonnaise.

INGREDIENTS

8	medium-size red apples, unpeeled and diced
2	tablespoons lemon juice
1	cup chopped celery
1	cup seedless green grapes, halved
1	cup chopped walnuts
½	cup raisins
1	cup mayonnaise
2	tablespoons sugar
1	teaspoon lemon juice
1	cup whipping cream
1	cup flaked coconut

DIRECTIONS

- Toss together diced apple and 2 tablespoons lemon juice in a large bowl.

- Add celery and next 3 ingredients to diced apple.

- Combine mayonnaise, sugar, and 1 teaspoon lemon juice in a small bowl.

- Beat whipping cream at high speed with an electric mixer until soft peaks form; fold into mayonnaise mixture. Stir in coconut.

- Fold mayonnaise mixture into apple mixture. Chill thoroughly.

Serves 16 to 20

Cancun Chicken Salad

INGREDIENTS

2   cups chopped cooked chicken breast

¼   cup chopped onion

¼   cup chopped red bell pepper

¼   cup sliced ripe olives

1   cup canned black beans, drained

1   cup (4 ounces) shredded sharp cheddar cheese

½   cup mayonnaise

½   cup sour cream

2   teaspoons fresh lime juice

½   teaspoon chili powder

½   teaspoon ground cumin

¼   cup chopped fresh cilantro

DIRECTIONS

- Combine first 6 ingredients in a large bowl.

- Combine mayonnaise and next 5 ingredients; add to chicken mixture, stirring well. Chill thoroughly.

Serves 6 to 8

This chicken salad is a favorite among our staff members. I always post the weekly menu on Tuesday morning, and I can usually hear them say, "Gosh, I hope we don't run out of it this time so I can have some." It is good served on a bed of lettuce with homemade tortilla chips surrounding the plate. We have also served it wrapped in a sun-dried tomato tortilla.

Apple-Romaine Salad

Crunchy romaine salad has been a popular side item, and this recipe uses the same dressing. The romaine lettuce, crunchy sour apple, cashew nuts, and wonderful sweet-and-sour dressing make this salad terrific.

INGREDIENTS

½   cup vegetable oil
½   cup sugar
¼   cup white wine vinegar
1½   teaspoons soy sauce
¼   teaspoon celery salt
      Pepper to taste
2   heads romaine lettuce, washed and torn
2   Granny Smith apples, unpeeled and diced
½   cup cashews, chopped

DIRECTIONS

- Whisk together first 6 ingredients.
- Toss together romaine, apple, and cashews in a large bowl. Pour dressing over mixture, and toss to coat. Serve immediately.

Serves 8 to 10

Lettuce is like conversation; it must be fresh and crisp, and so sparkling that you can scarcely notice the bitter in it.
-Charles Dudley Warner

Curried Cranberry-Chicken Salad

INGREDIENTS

2   cups chopped cooked chicken breast

1   medium apple, cut into ½-inch pieces

¾   cup dried cranberries

½   cup thinly sliced celery

¼   cup chopped walnuts

2   tablespoons chopped green onions

¾-1   cup mayonnaise

2   teaspoons fresh lime juice

¾   teaspoon curry powder

DIRECTIONS

- Combine first 6 ingredients in a large bowl.

- Combine mayonnaise, lime juice, and curry powder; add to chicken mixture, stirring well. Chill thoroughly.

Serves 4

This is a festive salad to serve during the holidays for lunch. It is a pleasant change from all the heavy winter food. We serve it on a bed of lettuce alongside Chilled Broccoli Salad and Lemon-Poppy Seed Muffins. It is also delicious on a croissant.

Marinated Green Bean and Sweet Onion Salad

Cilantro is one of my favorite herbs. Most people either love it or hate it. If you're not a fan, you can substitute chopped fresh basil in this wonderful summer salad. You can also use fresh, blanched green beans that have been sliced in half lengthwise and then cut into 1-inch pieces.

INGREDIENTS

2	cups canned whole green beans, drained
2	cups thinly sliced Vidalia onion
2	tablespoons chopped fresh cilantro
⅓	cup raspberry vinegar
3	tablespoons vegetable oil
2	teaspoons sugar
¾	teaspoon salt
¼	teaspoon pepper
4-5	cups torn leaf lettuce
½	cup chopped pecans

DIRECTIONS

- Combine first 3 ingredients in a medium bowl.
- Bring raspberry vinegar and next 4 ingredients to a boil in a saucepan, stirring constantly.
- Pour vinegar mixture over green been mixture and toss to coat. Cover and chill several hours.
- Place lettuce on individual salad plates. Using a slotted spoon, place green bean mixture on lettuce.
- Drizzle salad with additional marinade, if desired. Sprinkle with pecans.

Serves 4 to 5

Asian Grilled Chicken Salad

INGREDIENTS

½   cup vegetable oil

2   tablespoons oriental sesame oil

¼   cup sugar

½   cup rice vinegar

2   teaspoons soy sauce

1   teaspoon ground black pepper

½   teaspoon dried crushed red pepper

1   tablespoon chopped peeled fresh ginger

4   skinned and boned chicken breasts, grilled and shredded

1   large package coleslaw mix

1   (2-ounce) package slivered almonds

2   tablespoons sesame seeds

1   medium-size purple onion, thinly sliced

2   packages ramen noodles (discard sauce mix), broken into
      pieces

DIRECTIONS

- Whisk together first 8 ingredients in a large bowl.

- Add chicken to vinegar mixture and let stand 5 minutes.

- Add coleslaw mix and next 3 ingredients to chicken mixture, tossing well. Let stand 10 to 15 minutes.

- Add ramen noodle pieces, tossing well.

Serves 4

For a quick dinner, instead of grilling chicken breasts, try store-bought roasted chicken.

A la Carte Chicken Salad

INGREDIENTS

4	cups diced cooked chicken breast (still warm)
9	hard-cooked eggs, chopped (still warm)
1	cup chicken broth
2	teaspoons prepared mustard
2	tablespoons Durkee's mayonnaise-mustard sauce
2	tablespoons sugar
½-1	cup mayonnaise
¼	cup fresh lemon juice
3	cups diced celery
¾	cup sweet pickle relish

DIRECTIONS

- Combine chicken and egg in a large bowl.
- Add broth to chicken mixture, stirring well. Chill 30 to 60 minutes.
- Combine mustard and next 4 ingredients, stirring well.
- Add celery and relish to chicken mixture; gradually stir in dressing mixture.

Serves 10 to 12

Chicken salad has a certain glamour about it. Like the little black dress, it is chic and acceptable anywhere.

-Laurie Colwin

Nantucket Chicken Salad

INGREDIENTS

3½   pounds skinned and boned chicken breasts, cooked and cut into chunks

6   celery stalks, chopped

1½   cups seedless green grapes, halved

1½   teaspoons dried thyme

1½   teaspoons garlic powder

      Salt to taste

      Lemon pepper to taste

3-3¼ cups mayonnaise

DIRECTIONS

■   Combine first 3 ingredients in a large bowl.

■   Add thyme and next 3 ingredients to chicken mixture; stir in mayonnaise. Chill several hours.

Serves 6 to 8

A sophisticated classic, this chicken salad is a perfect luncheon dish in the hot summer months.

Maria's Cornbread Salad

INGREDIENTS

2	packages jalapeño cornbread mix
1	bunch green onions, chopped
1	bell pepper, chopped
2	tomatoes, diced
1	(16-ounce) can whole kernel corn, drained
1	cup (4 ounces) shredded cheddar cheese
8	bacon slices, cooked and crumbled
1½	cups mayonnaise
½	cup sour cream
½	teaspoon chili powder
½	teaspoon ground cumin
	Garnish: avocado slices

DIRECTIONS

- Prepare cornbread according to package directions. Let cool.

- Crumble cornbread into a large bowl; add green onions and next 9 ingredients, stirring well.

- Chill salad overnight. Garnish, if desired.

Serves 10

You've got to continue to grow, or you're just like last night's cornbread-stale and dry.

-Loretta Lynn

Fresh Cranberry-Apple Salad

INGREDIENTS

1½   cups fresh cranberries, coarsely chopped

3   tablespoons sugar

2   tablespoons fresh lime juice

2   teaspoons Dijon mustard

½   cup olive oil

1   cup chopped walnuts

2   large Granny Smith apples, unpeeled and coarsely chopped

¼   cup sliced green onions

1   head romaine lettuce, torn

DIRECTIONS

- Combine cranberries and sugar; chill overnight.

- Combine lime juice and mustard in a bowl; add oil in a slow, steady stream whisking constantly.

- Add walnuts, apple, and green onions to dressing and chill 1 to 2 hours.

- Line a serving platter or bowl with lettuce; spoon apple mixture over lettuce and top with cranberries.

Serves 6 to 8

This wonderful winter salad goes especially well with turkey. It's not bad in the summer either, if you remember to buy extra cranberries in the winter and freeze them.

Easy Seaside Tabbouleh

Last summer when we stayed in Florida, my sister-in-law Mary brought this fabulous Middle Eastern dish. I think it was meant to be a salad, but we inhaled it as a dip with water biscuits. Since then I have made it several times, and it tastes like summer to me-so fresh and crisp. It is good served as a side dish, as an appetizer, stuffed in a fresh tomato, or with pita bread.

I have included two versions of this recipe, super easy and from scratch. Take your pick.

INGREDIENTS FOR EASY TABBOULEH

1   package Near East tabbouleh wheat salad mix
1   diced tomato
     Juice of 1 large lemon
1   cucumber, peeled and finely diced
3   green onions, chopped
     Salt and pepper to taste
     Cavender's Greek seasoning to taste

DIRECTIONS FOR EASY TABBOULEH

- Prepare tabbouleh according to package directions; chill according to package directions.
- Add tomato and next 5 ingredients to tabbouleh, stirring well. Chill thoroughly.

INGREDIENTS FOR TABBOULEH FROM SCRATCH

2   pounds bulghur wheat
1½   cups fresh lemon juice
6   cups hot water
3   cucumbers, diced
8   small tomatoes, finely chopped
1   small purple onion, minced
2   garlic cloves, minced
3   bunches parsley, minced
5   tablespoons fresh mint, minced
1½   cups olive oil
     Salt and pepper to taste

DIRECTIONS FOR TABBOULEH FROM SCRATCH

- Place bulghur wheat in a large bowl; pour lemon juice and 6 cups hot water over wheat. Let stand 30 to 40 minutes.
- Drain wheat; add cucumber and next 5 ingredients, stirring well.
- Stir in additional lemon juice, if desired, and enough oil to moisten. Season with salt and pepper. Chill several hours.

Serves 14 to 16

Chilled Cherry-Pecan Salad

INGREDIENTS

12   ounces cherry-flavored gelatin

4   cups boiling water

2   cups crushed pineapple, undrained

2   cups cherry pie filling

2   (8-ounce) packages cream cheese, softened

2   cups sour cream

1   cup sugar

      Chopped pecans

DIRECTIONS

- Combine gelatin and 4 cups boiling water, stirring until gelatin dissolves. Let cool.

- Stir pineapple and cherry filling into gelatin mixture; pour into a 9 x 13 x 2-inch baking dish. Chill mixture until firm.

- Combine cream cheese, sour cream, and sugar in a bowl, stirring well. Spread over congealed mixture. Sprinkle with pecans.

Serves 12

Almost every person has something
secret he likes to eat.
                           -M.F.K. Fisher

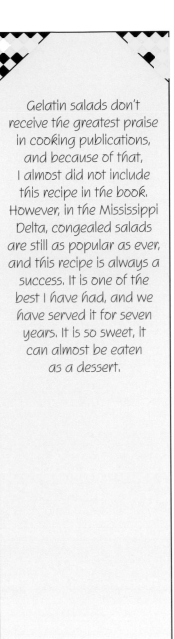

Gelatin salads don't receive the greatest praise in cooking publications, and because of that, I almost did not include this recipe in the book. However, in the Mississippi Delta, congealed salads are still as popular as ever, and this recipe is always a success. It is one of the best I have had, and we have served it for seven years. It is so sweet, it can almost be eaten as a dessert.

Chilled Broccoli Salad

This easy, delicious salad always receives compliments when we serve it. Cauliflower florets can be added for a change of taste. And the salad keeps well for several days.

INGREDIENTS

3	cups broccoli florets
6	bacon slices, cooked and crumbled
½	cup chopped purple onion
¼	cup shelled sunflower seeds
½	cup (2 ounces) shredded cheddar cheese
1	cup mayonnaise
2	tablespoons wine vinegar
¼	cup sugar

DIRECTIONS

- Toss together first 5 ingredients in a large bowl.

- Combine mayonnaise, vinegar, and sugar; pour over broccoli mixture and toss well. Chill thoroughly.

Serves 6

Simply Soups
& Bistro Breads

Soup Talk

Have you ever been confused by menu names or wondered what makes a soup a soup? Here's a quick description.

Bisque [bihsk]: a thick, rich soup usually consisting of pureed vegetables or seafood and cream

Bouillabaisse [BOOL-yuh-BAYZ]: a celebrated seafood stew from Provence, made with an assortment of fish and shellfish, onions, tomatoes, white wine, olive oil, garlic, saffron, and herbs

Bouillon [BOOL-yahn]: any broth made by cooking vegetables, poultry, meat, or fish in water. The liquid that is strained off after cooking is the bouillon, which can form the base for soups and sauces.

Broth: a liquid resulting from cooking vegetables, meat, or fish in water. The term is used synonymously with bouillon.

Chowder: any thick, rich soup containing chunks of food

Consommé [KON-suh-may]: a clarified meat or fish broth

Gumbo: a thick, stewlike dish that can have many ingredients, including vegetables such as okra, tomatoes, and onions, and one or several meats or shellfish, such as chicken, sausage, ham, shrimp, crab, or oysters

Soup: a combination of vegetables, meat, or fish cooked in a liquid. It may be thick, thin, creamy, or chunky.

Stew: a term most often applied to dishes that contain meat, vegetables, and a thick souplike broth resulting from a combination of the stewing liquid and the natural juices of the food being stewed

-from The Food Lover's Companion, 2nd edition,
by Sharon Tyler Herbst,
Barron's Educational Services, Inc.

Black-Eyed Pea Soup

"What??",
"Black-Eyed Pea Soup-
what in the world is that?",
and "Is it really good?"
are the comments we
usually hear while
answering the takeout
phone on Black-eyed Pea
Soup day. It is different,
and, yes, it is good. Even
though the soup is a little
spicy, it's not too much. It
needs a little kick to make
it interesting-right?

INGREDIENTS

1	medium onion, chopped
2	tablespoons bacon drippings
2	cups canned black-eyed peas, drained
1	cup beef broth
1	(10-ounce) can diced tomatoes with green chiles
½	cup (2 ounces) shredded sharp cheddar cheese

Salt and pepper to taste
Garnish: crushed tortilla chips

DIRECTIONS

- Sauté onion in hot bacon drippings in a large saucepan over medium heat until onion is tender.

- Mash peas and add to onion; add broth, diced tomatoes, and cheese, stirring well.

- Simmer soup until cheese is melted; season with salt and pepper.

- Serve soup hot and garnish, if desired.

Serves 4

All black-eyed peas are soulful.
-Marvalene Styles

Canadian Cheese Soup

INGREDIENTS

½   cup margarine

½   cup chopped onion

1   cup diced carrot

½   cup chopped celery

3 - 4 tablespoons all-purpose flour

3   cups chicken broth

3   cups half-and-half

2   (1-pound) processed cheese spread loaves, cubed

¼   teaspoon ground cumin

1   tablespoon chopped fresh parsley

Salt and pepper to taste

Garnish: diced fresh tomato, diced pickled jalapeño pepper

DIRECTIONS

- Melt margarine in a large saucepan over medium heat; add onion, carrot, and celery and sauté until tender.

- Reduce heat and add flour, stirring well. Cook, stirring constantly, until mixture begins to turn light brown.

- Increase heat to medium; gradually add broth, stirring constantly until mixture begins to thicken.

- Gradually add half-and-half, stirring constantly (do not let boil). Add cheese, stirring until melted.

- Add cumin and parsley and season with salt and pepper. Garnish each serving, if desired.

When we first started serving this soup, I think a lot of customers thought it was just going to be another ho-hum cheese soup. It didn't take long for word to spread that this soup is great. Now it always sells out, and usually before lunchtime is over. The waitstaff has declared it "awesome."

Fresh Mushroom and Rice Soup

It is still amazing to me how a few sprinkles of an herb can completely change the taste of a soup. Thyme is the secret ingredient in this recipe. Sometimes the rice absorbs a lot of the liquid, so add extra chicken broth, if needed.

INGREDIENTS

3	tablespoons butter
½	cup chopped red bell pepper
2	cups sliced fresh mushrooms
½	cup chopped green onions
1	tablespoon cornstarch
3½	cups chicken broth, divided
1	cup half-and-half
1	teaspoon dried thyme
1½	cups converted rice
	Salt and pepper to taste

DIRECTIONS

- Melt butter in a large Dutch oven over medium heat; add bell pepper, mushrooms, and green onions and sauté until tender.

- Combine cornstarch and ¼ cup chicken broth in a small bowl, whisking until smooth; set aside.

- Add remaining chicken broth and next 3 ingredients to vegetable mixture; bring mixture to a boil.

- Reduce heat and simmer, stirring often, 20 minutes or until rice is tender.

- Add cornstarch mixture and cook, stirring constantly, until soup is thickened.

Mushrooms are like men–the bad most closely counterfeit the good.
–George Ellwanger

Broccoli with Cheese Soup

INGREDIENTS

1	cup butter
1	cup all-purpose flour
1	cup chopped onion
1	cup chopped celery
1	pound broccoli, cut into florets
8	cups chicken broth
2	(1-pound) processed cheese spread loaves, cubed
½	pint whipping cream
	Freshly ground pepper to taste

DIRECTIONS

- Melt butter in a large Dutch oven over medium heat; gradually add flour, stirring constantly. Cook, stirring constantly, until roux turns brown. (Do not let burn.)

- Stir onion, celery, and broccoli into roux; gradually stir in chicken broth. Simmer, stirring often, 30 minutes or until vegetables are tender.

- Reduce heat and add cheese. Cook, stirring constantly, until cheese is melted.

- Stir in whipping cream and cook until thoroughly heated.

What would we do without tried-and-true favorites? If I had to choose which soup, out of all the ones we make, would win a "best-all-around" contest, it would be this soup. It's good in every season, and no one ever seems to tire of it.

The secret of staying young is to live honestly, eat slowly, and lie about your age.

—Lucille Ball

Cream of Mushroom Soup

INGREDIENTS

6	tablespoons butter
1	pound fresh mushrooms, sliced
1	onion, chopped
½	cup chopped celery
¼	cup all-purpose flour
3	cups chicken broth
2	cups half-and-half
¼	teaspoon dried tarragon
1	teaspoon salt
¼	teaspoon ground white pepper

DIRECTIONS

- Melt butter in a large saucepan over medium heat; add mushrooms, onion, and celery and sauté until tender.

- Add flour to mixture, stirring until smooth. Cook, stirring constantly, 1 minute.

- Gradually add broth and cook, stirring constantly, until mixture is thickened.

- Reduce heat and stir in half-and-half and next 3 ingredients. Cook soup until thoroughly heated.

Another basic recipe that is just plain good. Tarragon gives it a nice flavor.

What's a Wrap?

The wrap sandwich trend started in Berkeley, California, in the early nineties. It has taken a little time for the trend to move this far South, but in August 1998 we were the first restaurant in our area to put them on the menu.

Wraps are perfect sandwiches for today's get-it-and-go lifestyle. They are healthier than butter-laden sandwiches and can hold a wide assortment of fillings. To get started, you need a 10- or 11-inch flour tortilla and a good imagination. The sky is the limit as far as the ingredients you choose. Also remember that practice makes perfect. Follow these easy steps.

1. Decide on the filling.

2. Warm the tortilla slightly so that it doesn't tear.

3. Spread the filling in a 2 x 6-inch rectangle on the bottom half of the tortilla. Fold the right and left tortilla edges over the filling toward the center. Fold the bottom tortilla edge toward the center and gently roll until completely wrapped around the filling.

4. Enjoy your creation!

It was a struggle not to accept second or even third helpings of soup and to risk having no appetite left for the dishes to follow. This is one of the dangers of good soup.

-Elizabeth David

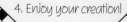

Curried Chicken Soup

INGREDIENTS

¼	cup butter
½	cup sliced fresh mushrooms
1	medium onion, chopped
3	red potatoes, peeled and chopped into small cubes
3	cups chicken broth
1½	teaspoons curry powder
¼	teaspoon ground cumin
1	tablespoon butter
1	tablespoon all-purpose flour
2	cups half-and-half
¼	cup dry sherry (do not use cooking sherry)
1	cooked chicken breast, chopped
	Salt and pepper to taste

Cumin and curry powder change this soup from ordinary to exotic. It is very aromatic, and I highly recommend it.

DIRECTIONS

- Melt ¼ cup butter in a large Dutch oven over medium heat; add mushrooms, onion, and potato and cook 10 minutes or until softened.

- Add broth, curry powder, and cumin to mixture; cook 30 minutes or until potato is tender.

- Melt 1 tablespoon butter in a small saucepan over medium heat; add flour, stirring constantly. Cook, stirring constantly, until roux turns brown. (Do not let burn.)

- Reduce heat and gradually whisk half-and-half into roux mixture; cook, stirring constantly, until blended and thickened. Add roux mixture to broth mixture.

- Add sherry and chicken to broth mixture and season with salt and pepper. Cook until thoroughly heated.

Chunky Baked Potato Soup with Cheese and Bacon

My idea of a perfect lunch on a cold Delta winter's day is a big bowl of baked potato soup with lots of toppings. The only problem is that it usually sells out before I get any! This is by far our best-selling soup. We keep increasing the quantity and we still sell out, so it must be good.

INGREDIENTS

½   cup butter

½   cup chopped onion

½   cup chopped celery

¾   cup all-purpose flour

5   cups milk

1¼   cups chicken broth

¾   teaspoon salt

½   teaspoon pepper

1½   cups (6 ounces) shredded cheddar cheese

4   large baking potatoes, baked, peeled, and cut into large chunks

12   bacon slices, cooked and crumbled

1   cup sour cream

     Toppings: chopped green onions, shredded cheddar cheese, crumbled cooked bacon

DIRECTIONS

- Melt butter in a large Dutch oven over medium heat; add onion and celery and sauté until tender.

- Add flour to mixture and cook, whisking constantly, 3 minutes. Gradually add milk and broth, stirring until thickened. Stir in salt and pepper.

- Add cheese to mixture and cook, stirring constantly, until melted. Stir in potato and bacon.

- Add sour cream and cook until thoroughly heated. Add desired toppings to each serving.

Serves 10 to 12

Corn Chowder

INGREDIENTS

½	cup butter
2	small onions, chopped
1	cup diced red bell pepper
1	teaspoon ground cumin
¼	teaspoon ground red pepper
½	cup all-purpose flour
2	cups chicken broth
2	cups milk
2	(16-ounce) cans whole kernel corn, with liquid reserved

DIRECTIONS

- Melt butter in a large saucepan over medium heat; add onion and next 3 ingredients and sauté until vegetables are tender.

- Add flour to mixture, stirring well. Gradually add broth, milk, and reserved corn liquid, stirring well.

- Bring mixture to a boil, whisking until smooth. Add corn, stirring well.

This Corn Chowder is not your ordinary corn chowder. It has a distinct Southwestern flavor. It's been on our rotating soup list since we opened.

When you are feeling sick . . . you want loving care and comfort. The foods that fill that need are simple, easy to eat, and cooked with love.

-Joyce Goldstein

Creamy Artichoke-Mushroom Soup

INGREDIENTS

¼	cup butter
¼	cup chopped onion
1	cup sliced fresh mushrooms
3	tablespoons all-purpose flour
1¾	cups chicken broth
2½	cups half-and-half
½	cup dry white wine
1	(14-ounce) can artichoke hearts, drained and chopped
½	teaspoon salt
	Dash of ground red pepper

DIRECTIONS

- Melt butter in a large saucepan over medium heat; add onion and mushrooms and sauté until tender.

- Stir flour into mixture; reduce heat and cook, stirring constantly, 2 minutes.

- Gradually add broth, half-and-half, and wine and cook, stirring constantly, until thickened.

- Stir in artichoke hearts, salt, and red pepper. Cook until thoroughly heated.

Serves 6

South of the Border Tomato Soup

INGREDIENTS

4	teaspoons butter
1	large onion, chopped
2	(28-ounce) cans Italian plum tomatoes
½	cup hot salsa
2	(8-ounce) packages cream cheese, cubed
3	cups chicken broth
2	cups half-and-half
	Juice of half a lemon
1	teaspoon hot sauce
2	teaspoons ground cumin
3	teaspoons chopped fresh cilantro
	Garnishes: thinly sliced lemon, chopped fresh cilantro

DIRECTIONS

- Melt butter in a large saucepan over medium heat; add onion and sauté until tender.

- Add tomatoes and salsa to mixture and simmer until liquid is almost absorbed.

- Gradually add cream cheese, stirring constantly until melted.

- Add broth and next 5 ingredients, stirring well. Cook until thoroughly heated.

- Serve soup warm and garnish, if desired.

Serves 8

This is my jazzed up version of cream of tomato soup. It is very rich, so it's good served with a green salad and French bread. I have always thought that it would be just as good served chilled in the summer.

New Potato Soup

Trying to come up with new soups that appeal to all sorts of customers is sometimes hard to do. Our baked potato soup has been such a good seller, that I wanted to do another variation that wasn't quite as heavy. We serve this more in the spring. The new potatoes give it a different texture, and the fresh basil is a nice flavor addition.

INGREDIENTS

1	cup butter
4	cups chopped onion
1	cup all-purpose flour
3	tablespoons chicken bouillon granules
1½	cups instant potato flakes
8	cups warm water
4	cups half-and-half
6	bacon slices, cooked and crumbled
2	teaspoons chopped fresh basil
2	dashes hot sauce
6	cups unpeeled boiled new potatoes, coarsely chopped

Garnishes: shredded cheddar cheese, chopped fresh basil

DIRECTIONS

- Melt butter in a large Dutch oven over medium heat; add onion and sauté until tender. Add flour and cook, stirring constantly, 2 to 3 minutes.

- Combine bouillon granules, potato flakes, and 8 cups warm water, stirring to dissolve; gradually whisk into flour mixture. Reduce heat and simmer 15 minutes.

- Gradually add half-and-half and next 4 ingredients; cook until thoroughly heated. Garnish each serving, if desired.

Serves 16 to 20

Vegetable-Tortellini Soup

INGREDIENTS

1   cup chopped carrot

1   cup chopped celery

1   onion, chopped

2   garlic cloves, minced

1   cup diced yellow squash

1   cup diced zucchini

6   cups chicken broth

2   large cans Italian-style whole tomatoes, diced

1   bay leaf

1   teaspoon dried basil

½   teaspoon dried oregano

1   teaspoon dried parsley

1   (16-ounce) package cheese-filled tortellini, cooked and drained

     Salt and pepper to taste

DIRECTIONS

- Stir-fry carrot and celery in a large Dutch oven coated with vegetable cooking spray, tossing constantly, 5 minutes; add onion and garlic.

- Add squash and next 7 ingredients to mixture and bring to a boil.

- Reduce heat and simmer 1 hour to 1 hour and 30 minutes.

- Stir in tortellini. Discard bay leaf. Season with salt and pepper.

Serves 8 to 10

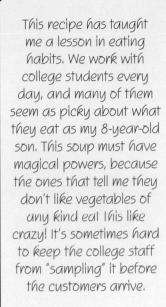

This recipe has taught me a lesson in eating habits. We work with college students every day, and many of them seem as picky about what they eat as my 8-year-old son. This soup must have magical powers, because the ones that tell me they don't like vegetables of any kind eat this like crazy! It's sometimes hard to keep the college staff from "sampling" it before the customers arrive.

Cream of Tortilla Soup

There must be a million tortilla soup recipes in print these days, so I hesitated about including this recipe. However, this one is a little different (and a little more fattening) than most.
We started serving this in 1992, and at that time a lot of customers had not heard of it. We now say that it is in our A la Carte Classic Hall of Fame.

INGREDIENTS

¼ cup butter

1 onion, chopped

2 garlic cloves, minced

½ cup diced celery

1 tomato, chopped

2 green onions, chopped

1½ cups tortilla chips, crushed

1 tablespoon all-purpose flour

4 cups chicken broth

¼ cup whipping cream

1 cup (4 ounces) shredded cheddar cheese

1 cup (4 ounces) shredded Monterey Jack cheese

2 teaspoons chili powder

2 teaspoons ground cumin

½ teaspoon hot sauce

Salt and pepper to taste

Toppings: crushed tortilla chips, chopped green onions, chopped tomato

DIRECTIONS

- Melt butter in a large saucepan over medium heat; add onion, garlic, and celery and sauté until tender.

- Add tomato, green onions, and crushed chips to mixture and cook 2 minutes.

- Reduce heat and sprinkle flour over mixture; cook, stirring constantly, 2 to 3 minutes.

- Gradually add broth, stirring well. Bring mixture to a boil.

- Reduce heat and stir in whipping cream.

- Gradually add cheeses, stirring until melted and well blended.

- Stir in chili powder and next 3 ingredients. Serve warm with desired toppings.

Serves 6

White French Onion Soup

INGREDIENTS

½   cup butter

2   cups thinly sliced onion

¼   cup all-purpose flour

1½   teaspoons salt

¼   teaspoon ground white pepper

4   cups milk

6   French bread slices (we used herbed garlic toast rounds), lightly toasted

6   Swiss cheese slices

     Freshly grated Parmesan cheese

DIRECTIONS

- Melt butter in a large saucepan over low heat; add onion and sauté, stirring constantly, 20 minutes.

- Add flour, salt, and pepper to mixture; cook, stirring constantly, until mixture is bubbly.

- Remove from heat and gradually stir in milk.

- Bring mixture to a boil, stirring constantly. Boil 1 minute.

- Place 1 toasted French bread slice in the bottom of each soup bowl; top each with 1 Swiss cheese slice.

- Ladle hot soup over bread and Swiss cheese and sprinkle with Parmesan cheese.

Serves 6

Traditional onion soup would be impossible for us to do correctly during the lunch hour. Gwen, our sandwich chef, is putting sandwiches under the broiler at lightning speed, and there is no way we would get a chance to melt the cheese on bowls of soup anywhere near her territory.

For that reason, I came up with a delicious variation, and we don't have to upset Gwen. It is extra creamy, and if it is occasionally too thick, we just add a little extra chicken broth to thin it.

Life is like an onion, you peel it off one layer
at a time; and sometimes you weep.
                    -Carl Sandburg

Corn, Rice and Smoked Sausage Soup

One day last winter when the temperature was below freezing, I had the good fortune to be able to play hooky from work. I was supposed to catch up on filing invoices and paying bills for the shop, but I felt like making a stick-to-your-ribs kind of soup. This is what I came up with. I tripled it and made a huge amount, so I took enough for our dinner and saved the rest to serve at lunch the next day at the shop. The flavors blended overnight, and it was even better.

INGREDIENTS

1	(6-ounce) package long-grain and wild rice mix
2⅓	cups chicken broth
6¼	cups frozen corn kernels, thawed
7½	cups chicken broth, divided
10	ounces fully cooked smoked sausage, cut into ½-inch cubes
2	tablespoons vegetable oil
3	carrots, diced
2	medium onions, chopped
1½	cups half-and-half
	Salt and pepper to taste
	Garnish: chopped green onions

DIRECTIONS

- Cook rice and 2⅓ cups broth in a saucepan over medium heat 20 to 25 minutes or until done.

- Process 3¾ cups corn and 1½ cups broth in a food processor until thick and almost smooth.

- Sauté sausage in hot oil in a large Dutch oven over medium heat 5 minutes; add carrot and onion and cook 3 minutes.

- Add remaining 6 cups broth to sausage mixture and bring to a boil. Reduce heat and simmer 15 minutes.

- Add cooked rice, corn puree, and remaining 2½ cups corn to soup; cook 15 minutes.

- Stir half-and-half into soup, adding additional broth if a thinner soup is desired.

- Season soup with salt and pepper. Garnish, if desired.

Serves 12

Red beans and ricely yours.
    —Louis Armstrong
(his sign-off on personal letters)

Red Bean Soup

INGREDIENTS

6	cups dried red beans
¾	cup butter
3	medium onions, chopped
9	garlic cloves, minced
1	cup chopped celery
6	quarts water
3	tablespoons Worcestershire sauce
3	bay leaves
3	teaspoons dried thyme
1½	pounds ham, chopped
	Salt and pepper to taste
1½	cups red wine
6	hard-cooked eggs, diced
3	lemons, thinly sliced

DIRECTIONS

- Soak beans in water to cover overnight; drain.

- Melt butter in a skillet over medium heat; add onion, garlic, and celery and sauté until tender.

- Combine sautéed vegetables, red beans, 6 quarts water, and next 3 ingredients in a large Dutch oven; cook, partially covered, over low heat 2 hours or until water is reduced by half.

- Strain bean mixture, reserving liquid.

- Process bean mixture in a food processor in batches, pulsing until smooth. Return bean mixture and liquid to Dutch oven.

- Add ham, salt, and pepper to mixture and simmer 10 to 15 minutes.

- Stir wine into soup. Top each serving with chopped egg and lemon slices.

Serves 20

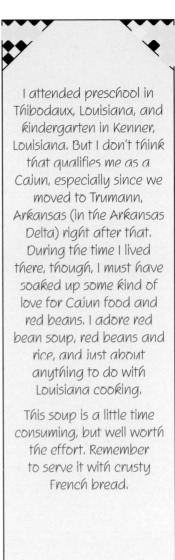

I attended preschool in Thibodaux, Louisiana, and kindergarten in Kenner, Louisiana. But I don't think that qualifies me as a Cajun, especially since we moved to Trumann, Arkansas (in the Arkansas Delta) right after that. During the time I lived there, though, I must have soaked up some kind of love for Cajun food and red beans. I adore red bean soup, red beans and rice, and just about anything to do with Louisiana cooking.

This soup is a little time consuming, but well worth the effort. Remember to serve it with crusty French bread.

The Art of the Sandwich

Customers ask almost everyday what makes our sandwiches so good? Well, it's a combination of things.

1. We use the highest quality bread, meat, cheese, and sauces.

2. We slice our own meat and cheese.

3. Gwen Carter is our sandwich chef. Gwen has making sandwiches down to a science. She is usually as cool as a cucumber in the kitchen, even when there are 50 orders hanging on the vent-a-hood above her head. She not only coordinates take-out and restaurant orders, but she also helps train the waitstaff about proper kitchen etiquette (first come, first serve- no one pushes an order in front of the other, write orders so that she can read them, and use proper manners- always say please and thank you).

(continued)

Roasted Eggplant Soup

INGREDIENTS

1	eggplant, about 7 inches long, unpeeled and cut into 1-inch slices
1	onion, cut into ½-inch slices
1	whole jalapeño pepper
1	red bell pepper, halved, seeds and stem removed
	Olive oil spray
2	tablespoons seasoning mixture
1	quart chicken broth
1	quart whipping cream
1½	sticks butter, melted
¾	cup flour
	Sour cream for garnish

SEASONING MIXTURE

- Combine equal amounts of garlic salt, basil, oregano, thyme and cayenne pepper.

DIRECTIONS

- Place eggplant, onion and peppers on a cookie sheet lined with foil. Bake at 425 degrees about 20 minutes until soft. Spray with olive oil and sprinkle with seasoning mixture. Turn vegetables during baking.

- Place slightly cooled vegetables into food processor and process until minced.

- In a large soup pot, add chicken broth and whipping cream. Heat until hot.

- Add vegetable mixture and cook on medium until heated through.

- Combine butter and flour to make roux.

- Add gradually to soup until desired consistency is achieved. (It should be thick.).

- To garnish, put sour cream into a squeeze bottle and squeeze some onto soup surface. Using a knife, cut across sour cream to decorate.

Yields 3 quarts

Black Bean Soup with Kielbasa

INGREDIENTS

8   ounces dry black beans (½ of a 16-ounce bag)
2   tablespoons olive oil
1   onion, chopped
1   red bell pepper, chopped
3   cloves garlic, minced
2   teaspoons chili powder
½   teaspoon cumin
¼   teaspoon oregano
     Pinch of cayenne
1   bay leaf
1   tablespoon brown sugar
5   canned plum tomatoes with 2 cups of the juice
9   cups water
½   pound Kielbasa, cut into chunks

GARNISH

1½   tablespoons chopped fresh parsley
½   cup chopped red onion
½   cup grated jalapeño Monterey Jack cheese
1   cup sour cream

DIRECTIONS

- Soak beans in cold water overnight. Drain and rinse.
- Heat olive oil in soup pot. Sauté onion and red bell pepper until soft. Add garlic and sauté for 30 seconds.
- Add the seasonings and cook for 1 minutes on low heat.
- Add sugar, tomatoes, tomato juice and water.
- Add drained beans and simmer for 1¾ hours or until beans are soft.
- Ladle the soup into the food processor in small batches and pulse. It should be a chunky purée.
- Return soup to soup pot and add kielbasa.
- Heat until warmed.
- Garnish soup with parsley.
- Have small bowls of other garnishes so that guests can garnish as they like.

Serves 4

She does 5,000 things at one time without getting flustered!

4. We use a commercial six-burner, two-oven stove, with a broiler unit that can't be beat.

5. Gwen makes the sandwiches a certain way. First she cuts and butters the bread, then she runs it under the broiler until browned. Next she pulls the bread out and puts the sauce, meat, and cheese on the sandwich. She then runs it back under the broiler to warm the meat and melt the cheese.

Just think about preparing several dozen sandwiches at one time in lightning speed and also making French fries and appetizers. She never misses a beat!

Summer Squash Bisque

We tried this recipe when the weather was starting to warm up and I was tired of putting heavy soups on the menu. It is another magical recipe, because people who claim they don't like squash usually like this.

INGREDIENTS

½   cup butter

1   medium onion, chopped

2   potatoes, peeled and cubed

2   carrots, diced

2   pounds yellow squash, sliced, or 2 packages frozen sliced squash, thawed

5¼   cups chicken broth

1   teaspoon ground white pepper

¼   teaspoon dried basil

1   garlic clove, minced

1   cup whipping cream

DIRECTIONS

- Melt butter in a large saucepan over medium heat; add onion and sauté until tender.

- Add potato and next 6 ingredients to onion and cook until potatoes are tender. Remove from heat.

- Process soup in a food processor in batches until smooth. Return to saucepan.

- Stir in whipping cream and cook until thoroughly heated.

Serves 8

Cheddar-Herb Biscuits

INGREDIENTS

2	cups biscuit mix
⅔	cup milk
1	cup (4 ounces) shredded cheddar cheese
¼	cup butter, melted
½	teaspoon garlic powder
¼	teaspoon salt
⅛	teaspoon onion powder
⅛	teaspoon dried oregano
1	teaspoon dried parsley

DIRECTIONS

- Preheat oven to 400 degrees.

- Stir together first 3 ingredients until a soft dough forms; beat with a wooden spoon 30 seconds.

- Drop dough by spoonfuls onto a greased baking sheet.

- Bake at 400 degrees for 10 to 12 minutes or until lightly browned.

- Combine butter and next 5 ingredients; brush over warm biscuits before removing from baking sheet.

Yields 12 biscuits

These biscuits taste similar to the ones served at several restaurant chains. I usually make them at home because my children are crazy about them.

"How long does getting thin take?"
Pooh asked anxiously.

-A.A. Milne

Broccoli-Cornbread Muffins

My mother's very special friend since childhood, Dot Kinman, shared this wonderful cornbread recipe with me a few years ago. It originally called for a 9 x 13 x 2-inch baking dish, but we bake it in muffin pans and serve it with a main-dish salad or quiche.

INGREDIENTS

2	(8½-ounce) packages Jiffy corn muffin mix
1	(10-ounce) package frozen chopped broccoli, thawed
4	large eggs, lightly beaten
1	cup cottage cheese
1	medium onion, chopped
1	cup margarine, melted
½	cup (2 ounces) shredded cheddar cheese

DIRECTIONS

- Combine first 6 ingredients in a large bowl, stirring until well blended.

- Pour batter into greased muffin pan cups; sprinkle with cheddar cheese.

- Bake at 375 degrees for 30 to 35 minutes or until lightly browned.

Miniature Parmesan Biscuits

INGREDIENTS

1¾   cups all-purpose flour

1   tablespoon baking powder

½   teaspoon salt

¼   cup grated Parmesan cheese

½   cup butter, cut up

½   cup milk

1   large egg

DIRECTIONS

- Preheat oven to 400 degrees.

- Combine first 4 ingredients in a large bowl; cut in butter with a fork or pastry blender until mixture is crumbly.

- Whisk together milk and egg; add to dry ingredients, stirring just until moistened.

- Spoon dough into lightly greased miniature muffin pan cups.

- Bake at 400 degrees for 10 to 12 minutes or until golden brown.

Yields about 2 dozen

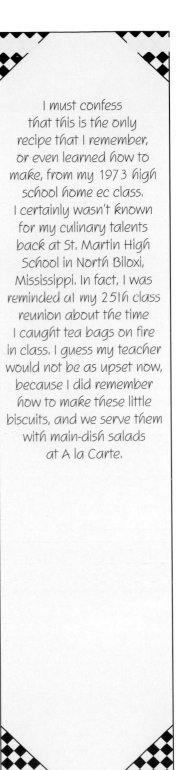

I must confess that this is the only recipe that I remember, or even learned how to make, from my 1973 high school home ec class. I certainly wasn't known for my culinary talents back at St. Martin High School in North Biloxi, Mississippi. In fact, I was reminded at my 25th class reunion about the time I caught tea bags on fire in class. I guess my teacher would not be as upset now, because I did remember how to make these little biscuits, and we serve them with main-dish salads at A la Carte.

Lemon-Poppy Seed Muffins

If you bake these muffins in miniature muffin pans, they look especially nice served for brunch or with a lunch salad. Baked in regular muffin pans they are a wonderful quick breakfast or snack.

INGREDIENTS

1	large egg
¾	teaspoon salt
⅓	cup sugar
¼	cup vegetable oil
1	cup milk
2	cups all-purpose flour
1	tablespoon baking powder
	Grated rind of 2 lemons
⅓	cup poppy seeds

DIRECTIONS

- Beat first 3 ingredients at medium speed with an electric mixer until light and fluffy.

- With mixer running, add oil in a slow, steady stream. Add milk, beating well.

- Sift together flour and baking powder several times.

- Add flour mixture, lemon rind, and poppy seeds to sugar mixture, beating well.

- Spoon batter into greased muffin pan cups. Bake at 400 degrees for 20 to 25 minutes.

Yields 12 muffins

A la Carte Cheese-Stuffed Garlic Bread

INGREDIENTS

1   cup (4 ounces) shredded mozzarella cheese

¼   cup mayonnaise

¼   cup butter, softened

1   garlic clove, minced

3-4 dashes dried parsley

1   French bread loaf, split lengthwise

DIRECTIONS

- Beat first 5 ingredients at medium speed with an electric mixer until blended.

- Spread cheese mixture on cut sides of bread. Place cut sides of bread together and cut into slices; or slice each half into 2-inch sections.

- Bake at 350 degrees for 5 to 10 minutes or until desired crispness.

Yields 1 loaf

Well, I did it! This is the recipe I have been trying to decide whether or not to put in the book. I kept thinking, "If I give away the recipe, maybe no one will buy it again." Because, you see, we keep this bread made up all the time to sell with our casseroles. I guess I'm taking a chance that many of you can enjoy making this at home, but when you are running short of time, you'll still buy some from me, right?

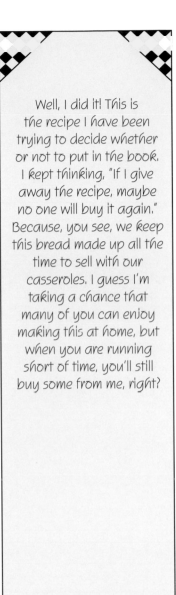

Black-Eyed Pea Cornbread

I made this cornbread recipe one New Year's Eve when we had a few friends over. That night I cut it into small squares and served it as an appetizer to jump-start having good luck for the coming year. It can be served as a side dish for a soul food dinner or as a main dish with a salad.

INGREDIENTS

1	pound spicy sausage
1	onion, chopped
1	cup white cornmeal
½	cup all-purpose flour
½	teaspoon baking soda
1	teaspoon salt
2	large eggs, lightly beaten
1	cup buttermilk
½	cup vegetable oil
1	(4.5-ounce) can chopped green chiles
¼	cup chopped pickled jalapeño pepper
¾	cup cream-style corn
2	cups (8 ounces) shredded cheddar cheese
1	(15-ounce) can black-eyed peas, drained

DIRECTIONS

- Cook sausage and onion in a skillet over medium heat, stirring until sausage crumbles and is no longer pink. Drain on paper towels.

- Combine cornmeal and next 3 ingredients in a large bowl.

- Combine eggs, buttermilk, and oil; add to dry ingredients, stirring just until dry ingredients are moistened (batter will not be smooth).

- Add sausage mixture, green chiles, and next 4 ingredients to batter, stirring well. Pour into a greased 9 x 13 x 2-inch baking dish.

- Bake at 350 degrees for 1 hour or until golden brown.

You just can't beat a woman
that looks city and cooks country.
-Granny, The Beverly Hillbillies

Daily Specials & Sides

Delta Chicken Vermicelli

INGREDIENTS

1	hen, boiled with broth reserved
3	large onions, chopped
3	bell peppers, chopped
1	large can mushrooms, with liquid reserved
	Vegetable oil
2	small cans tomato paste
2	cups water
5	cups canned tomatoes, chopped
1	can English peas, undrained
	Hot sauce to taste
3	teaspoons sugar
6-8	garlic cloves, crushed
½	small bottle Worcestershire sauce
1	pound sharp cheddar cheese, cubed
1	pound vermicelli, cooked
	Freshly grated Parmesan cheese

DIRECTIONS

- Debone chicken and cut meat into large pieces.

- Sauté onion, bell pepper, and mushrooms in hot oil in a skillet 10 minutes or until tender.

- Combine tomato paste and 2 cups water in a large Dutch oven, stirring well; add tomatoes, reserved mushroom liquid, and 4 cups reserved chicken broth. Bring mixture to a boil.

- Add onion mixture, English peas, and next 4 ingredients. Season to taste.

- Add chopped chicken and cubed cheese and cook, stirring often, until cheese is melted. Add hot, cooked pasta, stirring well.

- Transfer pasta mixture to a lightly greased 9 x 13 x 2-inch baking dish; sprinkle with Parmesan cheese.

Serves 10 to 12

When Mrs. Charlie Morlino gave me this recipe 15 years ago, never in a million years would I have thought I would use it so often. Nancy Jo, Mrs. Morlino's daughter, and husband Rusty invited me to join them for Sunday lunch at her parent's home. Mrs. Morlino had already earned the reputation as a good cook in Leland, Mississippi. But when she served this fabulous dish, I knew she was not just a good cook, she was a WONDERFUL cook. I thank her for sharing the recipe with me.

Chicken Enchiladas with Caramelized Onions and Roasted Red Peppers

When I was a teenager and a novice in the kitchen, I decided to impress my boyfriend by preparing a Mexican dinner for him and my family. I spent hours pouring over all my mother's cookbooks looking for the perfect menu. The grocery list was a mile long. The Saturday of the dinner, I woke up very early (giving up my sleep-time was unheard of in those days) and started preparing the dinner: beef enchiladas, refried beans, Mexican rice, and a salad. Dessert was some type of parfait with orange sherbet and raspberries (I wanted to use Mama's fancy parfait glasses). As I remember, it took me all day to get everything ready, and amazingly, it all turned out quite good. The only problem was that my father kept going on and on about how I had spent the whole week's grocery budget on one meal! He said, "Charlotte never wants to cook

(continued)

INGREDIENTS

2	tablespoons butter
2	large onions, thinly sliced
2	cups chopped cooked chicken breast
½	cup roasted sweet red peppers
6	ounces cream cheese, cubed
	Salt and pepper to taste
2	cups canned diced green chiles
½	cup chopped onion
2	garlic cloves minced
½	teaspoon sugar
1	tablespoon dried oregano
1	tablespoon ground cumin
1	(14½-ounce) can chicken broth
½	cup salsa
1	package flour tortillas
2	cups (8 ounces) shredded Monterey Jack cheese

DIRECTIONS

- Melt butter in a skillet over medium heat; add onion and sauté, stirring often, 20 minutes.

- Reduce heat to low; add chicken, red peppers, and cream cheese, stirring until blended. Add salt and pepper and remove from heat.

- Pulse green chiles and next 5 ingredients in a food processor several times to blend.

- Bring green chile mixture and chicken broth to a boil in a saucepan; boil 5 minutes or until slightly reduced (should be the consistency of a thin gravy). Add salt, if desired.

- Stir salsa into green chile mixture and remove from heat.

- Preheat oven to 375 degrees.

- Pour enough green chile sauce into a 9 x 13 x 2-inch baking dish to cover the bottom.

- Spoon ⅓ cup chicken mixture down the center of each tortilla and roll up; place seam side down in baking dish. Pour remaining green chile sauce over top and sprinkle with shredded cheese.

- Bake at 375 degrees for 20 minutes.

Serves 10 to 12

anything like tuna casserole or meat loaf; she wants to cook fancy." Now that I look back, it wasn't fancy at all; it was just simple food prepared in a different way and presented attractively.

This recipe is a little more complicated than the one I made then, but it is well worth the extra time.

Chicken-Wild Rice D'Iberville

INGREDIENTS

2	(3-pound) whole chickens
1	cup water
1	cup dry sherry
2	celery stalks
1½	teaspoons salt
1	onion, quartered
½	teaspoon curry powder
¼	teaspoon pepper
¼	teaspoon poultry seasoning
2	(6-ounce) packages long-grain and wild rice mix
½	cup butter
1	pound fresh mushrooms, sliced
1	bunch green onions, chopped
1	cup sour cream
1	(10¾-ounce) can cream of mushroom soup, undiluted
1½	cups crushed round buttery crackers
1	(6-ounce) can French-fried onions
¼	cup butter, melted
	Dash of garlic powder
	Dash of paprika

DIRECTIONS

- Bring first 9 ingredients to a boil in a large Dutch oven; boil 1 hour or until done.

- Remove chickens, reserving broth; let chickens cool. Debone chickens and cut meat into bite-size pieces; set aside.

- Pour chicken broth through a wire, mesh strainer, reserving enough to cook rice.

- Cook rice according to package directions using chicken broth, adding water to broth if necessary to reach needed amount.

- Melt butter in a skillet over medium heat; add mushrooms and green onions and sauté until tender.

- Combine hot cooked rice, chopped chicken, and sautéed vegetables in a large bowl; add sour cream and soup, stirring well.

- Pulse crackers and fried onions in a food processor until crushed. Transfer to a small bowl and stir in melted butter, garlic powder, and paprika.

- Pour chicken mixture into a greased 4-quart baking dish. Sprinkle with cracker mixture.

- Bake, covered, at 350 degrees for 15 to 20 minutes. Uncover and bake 5 to 10 more minutes.

Serves 12

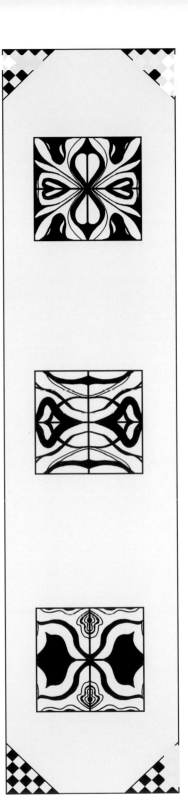

Poultry is for the
cook what canvas is for the painter.
-Jean-Anthelme Brillat-Savarin

Breast of Chicken Marsala

INGREDIENTS

6	skinned and boned chicken breasts
1	cup all-purpose flour
2	large eggs, lightly beaten
2	cups unseasoned fine, dry breadcrumbs
1	tablespoon butter
2	tablespoons vegetable oil
½	pound fresh mushrooms, sliced
2	tablespoons all-purpose flour
⅓	cup dry Marsala
1	garlic clove, minced
1	cup chicken broth
2	lemons, sliced
	Salt and pepper to taste

DIRECTIONS

- Dredge chicken in 1 cup flour, shaking off the excess thoroughly.

- Dip chicken in egg, and dredge in breadcrumbs.

- Melt butter and oil in a large skillet over medium heat; add chicken and sauté until golden brown. Remove chicken, reserving drippings in skillet.

- Add mushrooms to skillet and cook 1 minute. Sprinkle with 2 tablespoons flour and cook several seconds. (Do not burn.)

- Add Marsala and next 3 ingredients to mushrooms and cook, stirring often, until slightly thickened.

- Return chicken to skillet and season with salt and pepper. Cook, covered, over medium heat 10 to 15 minutes.

Serves 6

Catfish Margarite

INGREDIENTS

2   large eggs, lightly beaten

¼   cup water

1   tablespoon taco seasoning mix

½   teaspoon garlic powder

6   (6-ounce) catfish fillets

¾   cup all-purpose flour

1   (10-ounce) package tortilla chips, finely crushed

½   cup sour cream

½   teaspoon ground cumin

½   cup salsa

2   tablespoons chopped fresh cilantro

DIRECTIONS

- Whisk together first 4 ingredients in a shallow bowl.

- Dredge fillets in flour and dip in egg mixture; dredge in tortilla chips.

- Place fillets in a lightly greased baking dish. Bake at 375 degrees for 30 minutes.

- Combine sour cream and cumin, stirring well; chill.

- Combine salsa and cilantro, stirring well.

- Serve fish with a dollop of sour cream mixture and salsa.

Serves 6

One can't live in the Mississippi Delta and write a cookbook without including a few catfish recipes. This version of baked catfish has a distinct Mexican flavor.

Did you know that catfish was once classified as seafood's poor country cousin? Farm-raised catfish has now become one of the country's most popular and versatile foods.

If I go down for anything in history, I would like to be known as the person who convinced the American people that catfish is one of the finest eating fishes in the world.

    -Willard Scott

Parmesan Baked Catfish Fillets with Lemon Butter Sauce

This is my version of a recipe I found in a cookbook several years ago. We usually serve it as a daily special every other Friday, and it normally sells out before noon. There is a list we keep with names of customers to call on the day their favorite dish is prepared. Mr. and Mrs. F.H. Nance are on the list for this one. She says she loves it.

INGREDIENTS

1	cup crushed round buttery crackers
½	cup freshly grated Parmesan cheese
½	teaspoon dried oregano
¼	teaspoon dried basil
¼	cup chopped fresh parsley
½	teaspoon paprika
2½	teaspoons salt, divided
1	teaspoon pepper, divided
4	large eggs
4	tablespoons water
8	farm-raised catfish fillets
¼	cup butter, melted
1	cup butter, cut into fourths
½	cup fresh lemon juice
	Dash of Worcestershire sauce

DIRECTIONS

- Combine first 6 ingredients, 2 teaspoons salt, and ½ teaspoon pepper in a shallow dish.

- Whisk together eggs and 4 tablespoons water in a shallow bowl.

- Dip fillets in egg mixture and dredge in cracker crumb mixture.

- Place fillets on a greased pan and drizzle with melted butter.

- Bake at 350 degrees for 30 to 35 minutes.

- Simmer 1 cup butter, lemon juice, Worcestershire sauce, remaining ½ teaspoon salt, and ½ teaspoon pepper in a saucepan over low heat until butter is melted.

- Serve sauce over fillets.

Serves 8

King Ranch Chicken Casserole

INGREDIENTS FOR FILLING

2	whole chickens, boiled with broth reserved
1	cup chopped onion
2	tablespoons vegetable oil
1	(4.5-ounce) can chopped green chiles
1	(10¾-ounce) can cream of mushroom soup, undiluted
1	(10¾-ounce) can cream of chicken soup, undiluted
1	(16-ounce) container sour cream
1	(10-ounce) package frozen chopped spinach, thawed and well drained
1½	teaspoons chili powder
1	teaspoon dried oregano
1	teaspoon ground cumin
1	teaspoon salt
1	package corn tortillas
2	cups (8 ounces) shredded colby cheese

DIRECTIONS FOR FILLING AND ASSEMBLING

- Debone chicken and cut meat into bite-size pieces.

- Sauté onion in hot oil in a saucepan over medium heat until tender; add chiles and next 8 ingredients, stirring well. Set aside.

- Dip tortillas, 1 at a time, into reserved broth. Tear into large pieces and layer half in a 9 x 13 x 2-inch baking dish.

- Top tortilla layer with half each of sauce and chicken; repeat layers once. Sprinkle with cheese.

- Cover and chill at least 6 hours.

- Bake at 350* for 45 to 60 minutes or until cheese is melted.

Serves 6 to 8

A glass-front freezer in our small dining room houses all sorts of frozen casseroles that we prepare for customers to come in to buy or to have delivered to friends.

This dish is named for the largest modern-day ranch in Texas. It is very flavorful without being highly spiced. It's a favorite in the casserole freezer.

Seafood Gumbo Walton

First you make a roux . . .

This recipe comes from my brother Mark the "king" gumbo maker in our family. He lives on the Mississippi Gulf Coast and always has access to fresh shrimp and crab. He has made it so many times that now he never uses a recipe, and it always turns out fabulous. I could eat this everyday.

Mark's Gumbo Making Tips:

1. Make sure you have all your ingredients chopped and ready before you start your roux because you can't do all that chopping and tend the roux at the same time.

2. Great gumbo is not made in a hurry. One of the secrets of good gumbo is the roux, a mixture of flour and oil slow cooked in a heavy, cast-iron skillet. It is stirred as it cooks; otherwise, it becomes too hot and burns.

(continued)

INGREDIENTS

1	pound fresh crabmeat
5	pounds unpeeled, medium-size fresh shrimp
1	cup vegetable oil
1½	cups all-purpose flour
2	bell peppers, chopped
4	onions, chopped
8-10	celery stalks, chopped
6	green onions, chopped
10-12	garlic cloves, minced
1	(10-ounce) can chopped tomatoes and green chiles, undrained
3	(16-ounce) cans chopped tomatoes, undrained
1	tablespoon hot sauce
2	teaspoons salt
	Creole seasoning to taste
1	can beer
1	package frozen whole okra, thawed and rinsed
2	quarts water
3-4	bay leaves
	Hot cooked rice

DIRECTIONS

- Drain and flake crabmeat, removing any bits of shell. Peel shrimp and devein, if desired. Set crabmeat and shrimp aside.

- Heat oil in a large Dutch oven over medium heat until hot; gradually add flour, stirring constantly. Cook, stirring constantly, 30 to 45 minutes or until roux turns the color of a penny and develops a nutty aroma. (Do not let burn.)

- Add bell pepper and next 4 ingredients to roux, stirring well. Cook over medium heat 10 to 15 minutes until vegetables are tender.

- Bring chopped tomatoes and green chiles and next 8 ingredients to a boil in a large Dutch oven. Gradually add roux mixture, stirring until dissolved after each addition.

- Reduce heat to medium-low and simmer, stirring occasionally, 45 to 60 minutes.

- Gradually stir in crabmeat and shrimp; cover and cook until shrimp turn pink.

- Remove and discard bay leaves. Serve gumbo over hot cooked rice.

Serves 18 to 20

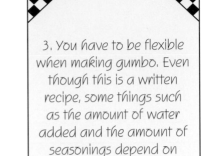

3. You have to be flexible when making gumbo. Even though this is a written recipe, some things such as the amount of water added and the amount of seasonings depend on how long your roux was cooked.

4. If making gumbo with fresh okra, cook it until it is no longer slimy, about 45 minutes, before adding other ingredients.

5. If using seafood in your gumbo, add it at the last minute so that it doesn't overcook.

Shrimp Creole Ocean Springs

It is interesting to me, thinking back, how many food memories I have that center around living on the Mississippi Gulf Coast. Fresh seafood was everywhere. My father would always get ours just as it had been caught, and he would usually buy 100 pounds at a time. Even though I dearly love shrimp, this was the one day of the year that I truly hated. I especially hated it when it interrupted my sunbathing time! He would summon my brother and me, and we would all have to sit under the carport and dehead all those shrimp; then we put them in freezer containers. We griped and grumbled; it was hot and the shrimp smelled. I would rather have done anything else but that. He always told us how fortunate we would be to have all this fresh shrimp to eat in the winter; it still didn't matter to us.

(continued)

INGREDIENTS

5	pounds unpeeled, medium-size fresh shrimp
¼	cup vegetable oil
¼	cup all-purpose flour
½	cup chopped green onions
2	cups chopped onion
2	garlic cloves, minced
1	cup chopped bell pepper
1	cup chopped celery
2	bay leaves
3	teaspoons salt
½	teaspoon pepper
1	(6-ounce) can tomato paste
1	(16-ounce) can chopped tomatoes
1	(8-ounce) can tomato sauce
1	cup water
	Dash of hot sauce
½	cup chopped fresh parsley
	Juice of ½ lemon
	Hot cooked rice

DIRECTIONS

- Peel shrimp and devein, if desired; set aside.

- Heat oil in a large iron skillet over medium heat until hot; gradually add flour, stirring constantly. Cook, stirring constantly, 30 to 45 minutes or until roux turns the color of a penny and develops a nutty aroma. (Do not let burn.)

- Stir green onions and next 7 ingredients into roux; cook over medium heat until onions are tender.

- Stir in tomato paste and cook 3 minutes. Stir in chopped tomatoes, tomato sauce, and 1 cup water and simmer, stirring occasionally, 45 to 60 minutes.

- Stir in shrimp and cook 5 minutes or until shrimp turn pink.

- Stir in hot sauce, parsley, and lemon juice. Cover and remove from heat. Let cool at room temperature to allow flavors to blend.

- Reheat shrimp mixture over medium-low heat and serve over hot cooked rice.

Serves 10

At the end of a good dinner, body and soul both enjoy a remarkable sense of well-being.
—Jean-Anthelme Brillat-Savarin

I guess something good did come out of all my duress-I can dehead and peel shrimp faster than anyone I have ever known since then. It's a good talent to have, especially since I love this recipe.

My husband is a meat-and-potatoes guy, so I sometimes have to use recipes for his kind of food so that he won't complain too much when I cook my kind of food. This is an excellent pork chop recipe; the gravy is wonderful. He likes it best served over fluffy white rice. I like it best served over lightly buttered noodles or orzo.

Pork Chops in a Brown Sugar Soy Sauce

INGREDIENTS

4   (1-inch-thick) boneless pork chops
1   garlic clove, minced
½   cup sherry (do not use cooking sherry)
½   cup soy sauce
¼   cup firmly packed brown sugar
¼   cup vegetable oil
2   dashes hot sauce
¼   cup cold water
4   teaspoons cornstarch

DIRECTIONS

- Brown pork chops in a heavy nonstick skillet lightly coated with vegetable cooking spray. Remove pork chops, reserving drippings in skillet.

- Add garlic to drippings and sauté until tender. Return pork chops to skillet.

- Combine sherry and next 4 ingredients, stirring well; pour over pork chops.

- Cover mixture and simmer 30 minutes or until pork chops are done. Remove pork chops from skillet and keep warm.

- Combine ¼ cup cold water and cornstarch in a small bowl, stirring until smooth. Add to sauce and cook until thickened.

- Serve sauce over pork chops.

Serves 4

Quiche Lorraine

INGREDIENTS

½   (15-ounce) package refrigerated pie crusts
      (we use Pillsbury refrigerated pie crust)

3   tablespoons butter

½   small onion, chopped

3   tablespoons chopped bell pepper

1   cup sliced fresh mushrooms

3   large eggs

1¼ cups sour cream

     Salt and pepper to taste

     Dash of garlic powder

     Dash of hot sauce

6   bacon slices, cooked and crumbled

1½ cups (6 ounces) shredded Swiss cheese

1   cup (4 ounces) shredded cheddar cheese

DIRECTIONS

- Fit pie crust into a 9-inch deep-dish pie plate; set aside.

- Melt butter in a skillet over medium heat; add onion, bell pepper, and mushrooms and sauté until tender.

- Whisk together eggs and next 4 ingredients until well blended; stir in onion mixture, bacon, and cheeses. Pour mixture into pie crust.

- Bake at 350 degrees for 35 to 40 minutes or until set and lightly browned on top.

Serves 6

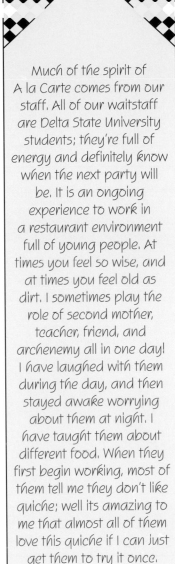

Much of the spirit of A la Carte comes from our staff. All of our waitstaff are Delta State University students; they're full of energy and definitely know when the next party will be. It is an ongoing experience to work in a restaurant environment full of young people. At times you feel so wise, and at times you feel old as dirt. I sometimes play the role of second mother, teacher, friend, and archenemy all in one day! I have laughed with them during the day, and then stayed awake worrying about them at night. I have taught them about different food. When they first begin working, most of them tell me they don't like quiche; well its amazing to me that almost all of them love this quiche if I can just get them to try it once.

Sweet-Spicy Chicken with White Barbecue Sauce

What a flavorful chicken dish this is! At first glance, the spice rub may seem a little overpowering, but the chicken absorbs just enough of the flavor. I love the white barbecue sauce. It looks a little different, but has a great taste. Cleanup tip: Line your baking dish with heavy-duty aluminum foil lightly coated with vegetable cooking spray—no dishes to scrub.

INGREDIENTS FOR CHICKEN

½   cup firmly packed light brown sugar

¼   cup chili powder

3   teaspoons salt

1   teaspoon pepper

1   teaspoon paprika

1   teaspoon garlic powder

6   boned chicken breasts

      White Barbecue Sauce

DIRECTIONS FOR CHICKEN AND ASSEMBLING

- Combine first 6 ingredients in a small bowl.

- Rub brown sugar mixture over chicken, patting with hand until thoroughly coated.

- Place chicken in a baking dish; cover with plastic wrap and chill 8 hours.

- Let chicken stand at room temperature 30 minutes. Place chicken, skin side up, in a shallow baking dish. Brush with reserved oil mixture from White Barbecue Sauce.

- Bake at 425 degrees for 20 to 25 minutes, basting occasionally. Serve with White Barbecue Sauce.

Serves 6

INGREDIENTS FOR WHITE BARBECUE SAUCE

1   cup chopped onion

½   cup vegetable oil, divided

2-3 garlic cloves, minced

2   tablespoons light brown sugar

1   tablespoon minced fresh parsley

½   teaspoon pepper

½   teaspoon salt

¼   teaspoon dried oregano

¼   teaspoon dried basil

½   cup white wine

¼   cup white wine vinegar

¼   cup butter, cut up

DIRECTIONS FOR SAUCE

- Sauté onion in 2 tablespoons hot oil in a saucepan over medium heat until tender.

- Stir in remaining 2 tablespoons oil and next 10 ingredients; reduce heat and simmer 30 minutes.

- Remove from heat and let stand at room temperature until fat rises to the top. Gently tilt pan and drain oil mixture from top; reserve for basting chicken.

- Process sauce in a food processor until smooth. Cook in saucepan over medium heat until thoroughly heated.

Yield 1 cup

Breast of Chicken Germaine

This easy recipe is delicious, and some of the preparation is done the day before. The chicken breasts marinate overnight in sour cream and seasonings. The next day the chicken is rolled in breadcrumbs and baked. It is a very good luncheon dish.

INGREDIENTS

2	cups sour cream
¼	cup fresh lemon juice
½	cup dry white wine
4	teaspoons Worcestershire sauce
4	teaspoons celery salt
2	teaspoons paprika
4	garlic cloves, minced
3	teaspoons salt
½	teaspoon pepper
12	boned chicken breasts
1¾	cups fine, dry breadcrumbs
½	cup butter, melted and divided

DIRECTIONS

- Combine first 9 ingredients; add chicken, tossing to coat well. Cover and chill overnight.

- Preheat oven to 300 degrees.

- Remove chicken from sour cream mixture and dredge in breadcrumbs, coating evenly.

- Arrange chicken in a single layer in a large baking dish. Drizzle half of butter over chicken.

- Bake at 300 degrees for 30 minutes. Drizzle remaining melted butter over chicken and bake 5 to 10 more minutes or until chicken is tender and browned.

Serves 12

To know about fried chicken you have to have been weaned and reared in the South. Period.
								-James Villas

Mexican Quiche

INGREDIENTS

5-6   medium eggs

¼   teaspoon salt

⅛   teaspoon ground nutmeg

¼   teaspoon ground red pepper

2   cups whipping cream

⅓   cup diced onion

⅓   cup diced tomato

⅓   cup canned chopped green chiles

1   (9 or 10-inch) unbaked pastry shell

½   cup (2 ounces) shredded cheddar cheese

½   cup (2 ounces) shredded Monterey Jack cheese

DIRECTIONS

- Whisk together first 5 ingredients until smooth and light in consistency.

- Sprinkle onion, tomato, and green chiles in the pastry shell; pour egg mixture over top. Sprinkle with cheeses.

- Bake at 375 degrees for 1 hour to 1 hour and 10 minutes or until a wooden pick inserted in center comes out clean.

- Let stand at room temperature 10 to 15 minutes before serving.

Serves 6 to 8

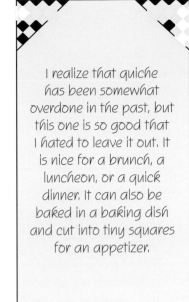

I realize that quiche has been somewhat overdone in the past, but this one is so good that I hated to leave it out. It is nice for a brunch, a luncheon, or a quick dinner. It can also be baked in a baking dish and cut into tiny squares for an appetizer.

Eating well gives spectacular joy to life.
               -Elsa Schiaparelli

Chicken Sauce Piquant

My mother and father, Aileen and Bill, have both made this Creole dish for years. When my mother makes it, she follows the recipe exactly. When my father makes it, he puts in everything but the kitchen sink! Surprisingly, both versions turn out terrific. This is a recipe Annie, a lady that helped my mother in the house, made when we lived in Thibodeaux, Louisiana. Mother said Annie made it using turtle meat, and that was the first time she had ever eaten turtle. I'm kind of glad my mother decided to substitute chicken when she made it.

INGREDIENTS

1   (3½ to 4-pound) whole chicken, cut up

       Salt to taste

1   cup shortening

2   quarts water

1   large can sliced mushrooms, with liquid reserved

3   green onions, sliced

2   cups chopped celery

1   green bell pepper, chopped

10   green olives, pricked with a fork

2   bay leaves

¾   cup all-purpose flour

2   large onions, finely chopped

4   garlic cloves, minced

1   large can tomato paste (about 12 oz.)

       Ground red pepper to taste

½   lemon, sliced

5   parsley sprigs, chopped

½   cup dry white wine

       Hot cooked rice or spaghetti

       Grated Parmesan cheese

DIRECTIONS

- Sprinkle chicken with salt.

- Melt shortening in a skillet over medium heat; add chicken and fry until browned. Transfer chicken to a large Dutch oven, reserving drippings in skillet.

- Add 2 quarts water, reserved mushroom liquid, and next 5 ingredients to Dutch oven and bring to a boil.

- Heat 1 cup reserved drippings in a heavy skillet over low heat; add flour and cook, stirring constantly, until dark brown.

- Add onion and garlic to browned drippings and cook, stirring constantly, until tender. Add tomato paste and cook, stirring constantly, until thickened and lumpy and the fat begins to separate.

- Add tomato mixture to chicken mixture and bring to a boil. Reduce heat and simmer, stirring occasionally, 1½ to 2 hours or until chicken is tender and sauce is thickened, adding water as needed.

- Add mushrooms, red pepper, lemon, and parsley; cook, stirring occasionally, 30 minutes.

- Stir in wine just before serving. Serve over hot cooked rice or pasta. Sprinkle with Parmesan cheese.

Serves 8

What Goes Where?

■ Forks go on the left, knives and spoons on the right; the knives positioned with the cutting side toward the plate.

■ No more than 3 pieces of silverware should be placed on each side of the plate.

■ Arrange the silver in the order it will be used, from the outside working in—if soup is your first course, put the soupspoon at the far right position. Dessert utensils should be positioned at the top of the plate—the spoon should be closest to the plate, the handle facing right; the fork above the spoon, facing in the opposite direction.

■ Glasses go on the right: the water glass directly above the knife, and the wine or other glasses to its right. The bread plate goes opposite the glasses, above the forks, with a butter knife sitting diagonally across the top of the plate. If a salad plate is used, position it to the left of the forks.

■ The water should be poured and candles lit when the guests sit down. Pour the wine after they're seated.

■ When serving food to seated guests, serve from the left; remove plates from the right. Since glasses are on the right side of a table setting, it's appropriate to pour beverages while standing to the right of your guest.

■ Pass food around the table in a clockwise direction (from right to left).

From "Never Eat More Than You Can Lift" by Sharon Tyler Herbst

Honey-Roasted Cumin Pork Tenderloin with Jalapeño-Onion Marmalade

This is an exceptional way to prepare pork tenderloin. We have done a version of it for special events, and the meat almost melts in your mouth. The sauce may seem a little intimidating at first glance, but it is not difficult and really complements the pork.

INGREDIENTS

¼	cup firmly packed light brown sugar
2	tablespoons ground cumin
2	teaspoons coarsely ground pepper
¼	cup balsamic vinegar
2	teaspoons Dijon mustard
2	garlic cloves, minced
	Dash of salt
1	pound pork tenderloin
½	cup honey
½	cup dry white wine
¼	cup Pickapeppa sauce
	Jalapeño-Onion Marmalade

DIRECTIONS

- Combine first 7 ingredients, stirring well.

- Place pork in a 9 x 13 x 2-inch baking dish and pour marinade over top. Cover and chill, turning occasionally, 6 to 8 hours.

- Preheat oven to 300 degrees.

- Drizzle pork with honey, wine, and Pickapeppa sauce.

- Bake at 300 degrees for 1 hour and 30 minutes.

- Slice pork and serve with Jalapeño-Onion Marmalade.

INGREDIENTS FOR JALAPEÑO-ONION MARMALADE

4	cups chopped Vidalia onion
	Salt and pepper to taste
3	tablespoons olive oil
2	fresh jalapeños, seeded and minced
2	tablespoons honey
3-4	tablespoons red wine vinegar
¼	cup water

DIRECTIONS FOR MARMALADE

- Season onion with salt and pepper to taste; sauté in hot oil in a skillet over medium heat until soft.

- Add jalapeño to onion and cook 1 minute. Add honey and cook 1 minute. Add vinegar and simmer, stirring constantly, until liquid is evaporated.

- Add ¼ cup water to skillet and simmer, stirring constantly, 10 minutes or until mixture is thickened. Season to taste.

In a quandary about tipping? You're not alone. Modern etiquette suggests that an appropriate tip range is 15% to 20% of the total bill before tax has been added. If the food or service is outstanding, however, you may want to tip more. But give some thought before you leave a small tip or none at all. If the food was inferior or slow in coming, the fault most likely lies in the kitchen and may be out of the waitstaff's hands.

–from **Never Eat More Than You Can Lift**, 1st edition, by Sharon Tyler Herbst, Broadway Books.

Chicken Longfellow Over Puff Pastry

This rich, elegant dish is served over puff pastry shells. We sometimes change the recipe slightly by adding a few English peas, steamed chopped carrots, and maybe some green beans. This changes it to a dressy version of chicken pot pie.

INGREDIENTS

3	tablespoons butter
2	cups sliced fresh mushrooms
½	cup butter
½	cup all-purpose flour
1	cup half-and-half
1	cup chicken broth
1	cup milk
2	cups diced cooked chicken breast
1	teaspoon salt
½	cup dry sherry
¾	cup slivered almonds, toasted
8	frozen puff pastry shells, baked

DIRECTIONS

- Melt 3 tablespoons butter in a skillet over medium heat; add mushrooms and sauté until tender.

- Melt ½ cup butter in a saucepan over medium heat; add flour, stirring until smooth. Cook, stirring constantly, 1 minute.

- Gradually add half-and-half, broth, and milk to flour mixture; cook, stirring often, until smooth and thickened.

- Fold mushrooms, chicken, and next 3 ingredients into milk mixture.

- To serve spoon chicken mixture over puff pastry shells.

Serves 8

Excellent wine generates enthusiasm.
And whatever you do with enthusiasm
is generally successful.
                                    -Philippe de Rothschild

Asparagus au Gratin

INGREDIENTS

3   tablespoons butter

¼   cup all-purpose flour

2   cups milk

¾   cup (3 ounces) shredded sharp cheddar cheese

½   teaspoon salt

       Dash of paprika

2   cans asparagus, drained

2   hard-cooked eggs, sliced

1   cup buttered breadcrumbs

DIRECTIONS

- Melt butter in a saucepan over medium heat; add flour, stirring until smooth. Gradually add milk, stirring constantly until thickened. Add cheese, stirring until melted.

- Remove from heat and stir in salt and paprika.

- Pour one-third of white sauce into a buttered baking dish; top with half each of asparagus and egg. Repeat layers with remaining sauce, asparagus, and egg, ending with sauce. Top with breadcrumbs.

- Bake at 350 degrees for 1 hour.

Serves 6

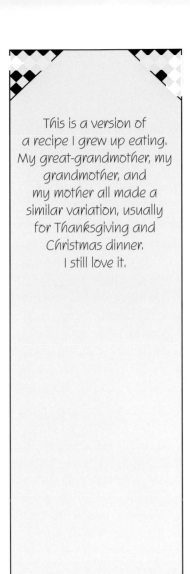

This is a version of a recipe I grew up eating. My great-grandmother, my grandmother, and my mother all made a similar variation, usually for Thanksgiving and Christmas dinner. I still love it.

Food has a rare ability to carry you back. . . .
[it] can be counted on to produce a
sensation in time present that will duplicate
a sensation from time past.

-Michael Frank

Shrimp and Crab Mornay

I remember distinctly the first time I tasted this dish. I was working in a department store in Pascagoula, Mississippi, and we were having a Christmas party. One of my coworkers brought this creation, which she served in a chafing dish as an hors d'oeuvre. The first bite I took made me feel as if I were in heaven. All of my favorite ingredients in one dish!

Eighteen years later, I still have the recipe she hastily wrote on a scrap of paper for me. This versatile recipe can also be cooked in a saucepan and served over pasta or pastry shells. It can be a main dish or served in a chafing dish with Melba rounds. Any way it is prepared, it is absolutely delicious.

INGREDIENTS

½	cup butter
½	cup all-purpose flour
¼	cup grated onion
½	cup chopped green onions
2	tablespoons chopped fresh parsley
2	cups whipping cream
1	cup dry white wine
1	teaspoon salt
½	teaspoon ground white pepper
¼	teaspoon ground red pepper
½	cup (2 ounces) shredded Swiss cheese
2	(6½-ounce) jars marinated artichoke hearts, drained and chopped
2	tablespoons fresh lemon juice
1	pound lump crabmeat, drained and picked over
1½	pounds medium fresh shrimp, boiled, peeled, and deveined, if desired
2	cups sliced fresh mushrooms
3	tablespoons freshly grated Romano cheese

DIRECTIONS

- Melt butter in a large saucepan over medium heat; gradually stir in flour. Cook, stirring constantly, 5 minutes.

- Add onions to flour mixture and cook 2 to 3 minutes. Stir in parsley.

- Gradually stir cream into flour mixture, and cook until thoroughly heated. Stir in wine and next 3 ingredients. Simmer, stirring occasionally.

- Add Swiss cheese to cream mixture, stirring until melted. Cover and remove from heat. Let cool.

- Fold in artichoke hearts and next 4 ingredients. Pour mixture into a greased 3-quart baking dish. Sprinkle with Romano cheese.

- Chill casserole in order for flavors to blend, if desired. Let stand at room temperature 30 minutes before baking.

- Bake at 350 degrees for 30 to 45 minutes or until golden brown. Broil a few minutes to brown top, if necessary.

Sweet and Sour Green Beans

INGREDIENTS

4   (16-ounce) cans whole green beans, drained

2   medium onions, sliced and separated into rings

16 bacon slices

¾   cup firmly packed light brown sugar

¾   cup vinegar

DIRECTIONS

- Place green beans in a 3-quart baking dish; place onion slices over beans.

- Fry bacon in a skillet over medium heat until crisp; drain, reserving drippings. Crumble bacon and sprinkle over onion.

- Cook reserved bacon drippings, brown sugar, and vinegar in skillet over medium-low heat until sugar is dissolved.

- Pour sugar mixture over casserole and chill several hours.

- Bake at 325 degrees for 1 hour.

Serves 8

I realize that versions of this recipe have been around a long time, but customers still comment on how wonderful these green beans are. Try not to think about the bacon grease; it's not good for you, but it gives the dish such a great flavor.

One cup slivered almonds can also be added for extra crunch.

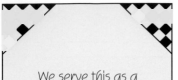

Green Beans Dijon

INGREDIENTS

½   cup mayonnaise

½   cup sour cream

3   tablespoons Dijon mustard

1   teaspoon garlic salt

1   garlic clove, minced

1   tablespoon Worcestershire sauce

2   (16-ounce) cans whole green beans, drained

½   cup pecans, chopped

DIRECTIONS

- Combine first 6 ingredients, stirring well.

- Place beans in a lightly greased baking dish, and cover with mayonnaise mixture.

- Bake at 350 degrees for 15 minutes. Sprinkle with pecans, and bake 10 more minutes.

Serves 8

We serve this as a side dish with several of our daily specials. It is a terrific recipe and very simple to make.

Remember when you were a child and your mom wouldn't let you leave the dinner table until you ate all your Brussels sprouts, and so you took your fork and mashed them into smaller and smaller pieces in hopes of eventually reducing them to individual Brussels sprouts molecules that would be absorbed into the atmosphere and disappear?

-Dave Barry

Broccoli Soufflé

INGREDIENTS

4   large eggs

1   (10-ounce) package frozen chopped broccoli, thawed and drained

1   cup (4 ounces) shredded cheddar cheese

1   cup mayonnaise

1   (10¾-ounce) can cream of mushroom soup, undiluted

DIRECTIONS

- Whisk eggs in a large bowl until light and fluffy; fold in broccoli and next 3 ingredients.

- Pour mixture into a lightly greased 1½-quart soufflé dish.

- Place soufflé dish in a large pan; add hot water to pan to a depth of 2 inches.

- Bake at 350 degrees for 1 hour or until a knife inserted in center comes out clean.

Serves 6

Occasionally you find a recipe that is so easy, so flexible, and loved by almost everyone. At A la Carte, it's the Broccoli Soufflé. We've been serving it as a side dish for seven years now. For a variation you can substitute 1 (15½-ounce) can asparagus, drained, or 1 (10-ounce) package frozen chopped spinach, thawed and well drained, for broccoli. One basic recipe-three casseroles.

A la Carte Spinach-Cheese Casserole

INGREDIENTS

2   (24-ounce) containers cottage cheese

2   pounds sharp cheddar cheese, shredded

6   large eggs, lightly beaten

½   cup butter, melted

2   (10-ounce) packages frozen chopped spinach, cooked and well drained

2   tablespoons Worcestershire sauce

6   tablespoons all-purpose flour

     Cavender's Greek seasoning to taste

     Garlic powder to taste

DIRECTIONS

- Combine all ingredients in a large bowl, stirring well.

- Pour mixture into a lightly greased 9 x 13 x 2-inch baking dish.

- Bake at 350 degrees for 1 hour.

Serves 12

I have never been a so-called finicky eater, but at one time in my life I really did not care much for cooked spinach. This was the first spinach dish I ever tried that I really liked, and it converted me to a full-fledged spinach lover.

This recipe can also be halved and baked in a deep-dish pie crust for a luncheon entrée. It can be made a day ahead and chilled overnight.

Life and living aren't the same. Life is more than just drawing breath.

-Elvis

Spinach Rockefeller in Tomato Cups

INGREDIENTS

12	medium tomatoes
	Garlic salt to taste
2	(10-ounce) packages frozen chopped spinach, cooked and well drained
2	cups fine, dry breadcrumbs
1	medium onion, diced
1	garlic clove, crushed
6	large eggs, lightly beaten
¾	cup butter, melted
½	cup grated Parmesan cheese
½	teaspoon ground black pepper
¼-½	teaspoon ground red pepper
	Salt to taste

DIRECTIONS

- Scoop pulp from tomatoes and discard; sprinkle inside of tomato shells with garlic salt and set aside.

- Combine spinach and next 9 ingredients; spoon mixture evenly into tomato shells.

- Place tomatoes on lightly greased baking sheets. Bake at 325 degrees for 15 minutes.

Serves 12

After I discovered spinach wasn't so bad, I suddenly began trying all sorts of spinach recipes. This one has an excellent flavor and makes an attractive side dish. For an hors d'oeuvre, stuff hollowed cherry tomatoes with this filling, and serve on a pretty platter.

But for a no-spinach version to serve to those who haven't been converted, combine 1 cup sour cream, ½ teaspoon salt, ¼ teaspoon pepper, 1 teaspoon sugar, 2 tablespoons all-purpose flour, 2 tablespoons minced onion, and 2 tablespoons chopped green chiles; spoon into hollowed tomatoes. Broil 4 inches from heat 3 to 4 minutes or until bubbly. Top evenly with 1 cup shredded cheddar cheese and ½ cup shredded Monterey Jack cheese. Broil 1 to 2 minutes or until lightly browned.

Huntington Sweet Potato Casserole

INGREDIENTS

4	large sweet potatoes (2 cups cooked)
1	cup firmly packed light brown sugar, divided
½	cup butter, softened
½	cup granulated sugar
¼	cup milk
½	teaspoon ground nutmeg
½	teaspoon ground cinnamon
1	teaspoon vanilla extract
1	teaspoon freshly grated orange rind
2	tablespoons amaretto
2	large eggs
1	small can mandarin oranges, drained
⅓	cup butter, melted
¾	cup chopped pecans
1	cup crushed cornflakes cereal (optional)

DIRECTIONS

- Boil sweet potatoes in water to cover 45 to 60 minutes; peel and mash.

- Beat sweet potato, ½ cup brown sugar, and next 9 ingredients at medium speed with an electric mixer until blended. Fold in mandarin oranges.

- Pour mixture into a lightly greased baking dish.

- Bake at 350 degrees for 25 to 30 minutes.

- Combine remaining ½ cup brown sugar, melted butter, pecans, and, if desired, cornflakes.

- Remove casserole from oven and top with cornflakes mixture. Bake 5 more minutes or until topping is browned.

Magnolia Squash Casserole

INGREDIENTS

2	pounds yellow squash, sliced (about 6 medium)
1	cup water
4	tablespoons butter
½	cup (2 ounces) shredded cheddar cheese
1	cup sour cream
6	green onions, chopped
½	cup freshly grated Parmesan cheese
1	cup buttered breadcrumbs

DIRECTIONS

- Cook squash in 1 cup water and seasoning of choice 15 minutes; drain and stir in butter.

- Add cheddar cheese and next 3 ingredients to squash, stirring well. Season to taste.

- Pour mixture into a lightly greased baking dish. Top with breadcrumbs and bake at 350 degrees for 30 minutes or until bubbly.

Serves 6 to 8

While attending college at Mississippi University for Women, my favorite vegetable served in the dorm dining room was squash casserole. This isn't the exact recipe Magnolia dining room used, but it is similar.

Summer cooking implies a sense of immediacy, a capacity to capture the essence of a fleeting moment.
-Elizabeth David

Twice-Baked Potatoes

It's hard to improve on a basic baked potato with all the trimmings, but I think this recipe tops it. We usually serve it with Parmesan Baked Catfish Fillets at lunch. These potatoes are popular with both customers and our staff. The waitstaff sometimes begs the kitchen staff to make a few extra so they can have a taste. You know how "starving" college students are!

INGREDIENTS

4   baking potatoes
1   cup (4 ounces) shredded cheddar cheese, divided
⅓   stick butter
¼   cup sour cream
3-4   tablespoons milk
       Salt and pepper to taste
½   pound bacon, cooked and crumbled
¼   cup chopped green onions

DIRECTIONS

- Bake potatoes wrapped in aluminum foil at 400 degrees for 45 to 60 minutes or until tender. Let cool 20 minutes.

- Cut potatoes in half lengthwise and scoop pulp into a bowl.

- Mash pulp and stir in ½ cup cheese and next 4 ingredients. Spoon evenly into potato shells.

- Place potato shells on a baking sheet and top evenly with remaining ½ cup cheese, bacon, and green onions.

- Bake at 350 degrees for 10 to 12 minutes or until cheese melts.

Serves 8

My idea of heaven is a great big baked potato and someone to share it with.

-Oprah Winfrey

Oven-Roasted Vidalia Onions and New Potatoes

INGREDIENTS

10-12	new potatoes, unpeeled, washed, and halved
3	Vidalia onions, cut into quarters
½	cup olive oil
1½	teaspoons kosher salt
1	teaspoon garlic powder
1	teaspoon lemon pepper
1	teaspoon dried oregano
½	teaspoon dried basil
1	teaspoon paprika
1	teaspoon Cavender's Greek seasoning
⅓	cup balsamic vinegar
⅓	cup white wine

DIRECTIONS

- Place potato halves and onion in a lightly greased baking dish.

- Combine oil and next 9 ingredients, stirring well; pour over potato and onion, tossing to coat well.

- Bake at 375 degrees for 1 hour and 15 minutes or until potato halves are crisp and done.

Serves 6

I love the rustic look and flavor of these onions and potatoes, kind of an updated comfort food. This dish is good served with steak, pork tenderloin, baked fish, roast, and chicken.

Another easy version of roasted potatoes is to toss together halved new potatoes and ¹/₂ cup pesto. Spread them on a baking sheet and bake at 400 degrees for 45 minutes or until crisp.

Potatoes are to food what
sensible shoes are to fashion.
-Linda Wells

Arkansas Cornbread Dressing

Since I have been in the restaurant business, I've learned that the type of cornbread dressing a person likes is sometimes as personal as his favorite color. There are hundreds of versions, and everyone likes his version best.

My father always made the dressing at our house, and because we lived on the Gulf Coast, it usually contained oysters. My husband's family and my own children would never dream of such a thing. I stick to the basic recipe my father uses, without all the embellishments. Even though most of you probably have a favorite dressing recipe, I included this one because it is a little different (and after all, my roots are in Arkansas). It belongs to my Aunt Nancy, and she got it many years ago from her Aunt Dude. My uncle and my cousins swear by it.

INGREDIENTS FOR DRESSING

	Cornbread (hot)
1	white bread loaf
	Turkey broth
4	large eggs, lightly beaten
2	medium onions, chopped
1½	cups chopped celery
	Poultry seasoning to taste
1	teaspoon coarsely ground black pepper
1	cup butter, melted
1	package slivered almonds

DIRECTIONS FOR DRESSING

- Crumble hot cornbread and white bread in a large bowl; stir in enough turkey broth to soften.

- Add eggs and next 6 ingredients to bread mixture, stirring well and adding additional bread if too thin.

- Transfer mixture to a lightly greased 9 x 13 x 2-inch pan. Bake at 350 degrees until golden brown.

INGREDIENTS FOR CORNBREAD

3	large eggs
2	cups buttermilk
2	cups plain cornmeal
½	teaspoon baking soda
2	teaspoons baking powder
½	teaspoon salt
2	tablespoons sugar
1	cup butter, melted

Arkansas Cornbread Dressing continued

DIRECTIONS FOR CORNBREAD

- Whisk eggs in a large bowl. Stir in buttermilk.

- Combine cornmeal and next 4 ingredients; stir into buttermilk mixture. Stir in butter.

- Pour batter into a hot greased large skillet. Bake at 350 degrees until golden brown.

Bill's Turkey in a Sack
(my father's method)

1 (10-12 pound) turkey
1 cup peanut oil
5 tablespoons paprika
2 tablespoons warm water
  Salt and pepper to taste
1 large brown paper grocery bag (hole free)

- In a bowl, combine paprika and warm water. Mix well until there are no lumps. Add oil and mix well.

- Using your hands, completely baste the turkey with the peanut oil mixture, both inside and outside of bird.

- Place turkey on an aluminum pie pan, breast-side up. Pour remainder of peanut oil mixture into the brown bag and swish around until the bag is completely saturated (a little more peanut oil may be needed).

- Place the turkey on the pie pan into the paper bag. Staple the bag shut.

- Place entire bag containing the turkey and pie pan in a roasting pan and bake in a pre-heated 325-degree oven for about 10 minutes per pound. Do not let the bag touch the top or sides of the oven.

Super Simple Baked Corn

Simple is sometimes best, and this dish is just that. This is the corn recipe we serve in the restaurant. It was given to me by Mrs. James Shepherd, one of the best cooks in Sunflower County.

INGREDIENTS

½   cup butter, melted
1   (14.75-ounce) can cream-style corn
1   (15.25-ounce) can whole kernel corn, drained
1   cup sour cream
1   box Jiffy cornbread mix

DIRECTIONS

- Combine all ingredients, stirring well.
- Pour mixture into a lightly greased 9-inch square baking dish.
- Bake at 350 degrees for 40 minutes or until golden brown.

Serves 8

Some people's food always tastes better than others, even if they are cooking the same dish at the same dinner . . . because one person has more life in them-more fire, more vitality, more guts-than others. A person without these things can never make food taste right, no matter what materials you give them. . . . they have nothing in themselves to give. You have got to throw feeling into cooking.

—Rosa Lewis

Pineapple Soufflé

INGREDIENTS

4   cups torn croissants

1   (20-ounce) can crushed pineapple, drained

3   large eggs, lightly beaten

2   cups sugar

1   cup butter, melted

1   teaspoon vanilla extract

DIRECTIONS

- Combine croissant pieces and pineapple in a large bowl.

- Spoon mixture into a lightly greased 2-quart rectangular baking dish.

- Combine eggs and next 3 ingredients, stirring well. Pour over bread mixture.

- Bake at 350 degrees for 30 minutes.

Serves 4 to 6

This is a very rich, very sweet side dish that goes well with ham, turkey, and chicken. Almost every time we serve it, I get requests for the recipe. I always answer the same, "Someday I am going to write a cookbook and it will be in there." So to everyone I have told that, I happily share the recipe.

Dreams, if they're any good,
are always a little crazy.
-Ray Charles

Mack's Tomato Pie

INGREDIENTS

1   9-inch unbaked pastry shell
    (we use Pillsbury refrigerated pie crust)

3   large tomatoes, chopped and drained

1   cup mayonnaise

1   cup (4 ounces) shredded sharp cheddar cheese

½   teaspoon salt

½   teaspoon pepper

½   teaspoon dried oregano

½   teaspoon dried basil

3   teaspoons chopped fresh parsley

DIRECTIONS

- Prebake pastry shell 10 minutes according to package directions.

- Place chopped tomato in pastry shell.

- Combine mayonnaise and next 6 ingredients; spoon over tomato.

- Bake at 350 degrees for 25 to 35 minutes.

Serves 6 to 8

My brother-in-law Mack is known in the Skelton family for his cooking ability. His wife, Jane, kindly shared this recipe with me. She said that Mack always adds extra ingredients when he's cooking, and his special touches for this dish are a little cumin, minced garlic, and a sprinkle of dill.

This pie makes a nice luncheon entrée or a side dish served with grilled meat. Juicy, vine-ripened tomatoes and fresh basil make it even better.

Indulgences

WHOLE PIES FOR
SALE

CARAMEL ALMOND....$ 14.00

FROZEN SNICKERS....$ 14.00

COBBLERS
FOR SALE
(TURN POP IN THE OVEN AND BAKE
SERVES APPROX. 10.)
CHERRY........$18.00
BLACKBERRY..$ 18.00
STRAWBERRY..$18.00
PECAN............$20.00

Mom-mo's Swedish Pineapple Cake

INGREDIENTS FOR CAKE

2	large eggs
2	cups sugar
1	(20-ounce) can crushed pineapple, undrained
1	teaspoon vanilla extract
2	cups all-purpose flour
2	teaspoons baking soda
½	teaspoon salt
½	cup chopped pecans
	Frosting
	Additional chopped pecans

DIRECTIONS FOR CAKE

- Beat eggs at medium speed with an electric mixer until fluffy; add sugar and beat until thickened.
- Add pineapple and next 5 ingredients to mixture, beating well.
- Pour batter into a lightly greased 9 x 13 x 2-inch pan.
- Bake at 350 degrees for 40 to 45 minutes. Let cool in pan on a wire rack.
- Spread Frosting over cake and sprinkle with chopped pecans.

INGREDIENTS FOR FROSTING

2	cups sifted powdered sugar, sifted
1	(8-ounce) package cream cheese, softened
¼	cup butter, softened
1	teaspoon vanilla extract

DIRECTIONS FOR FROSTING

- Beat all ingredients at medium speed with an electric mixer until creamy.

Serves 10 to 12

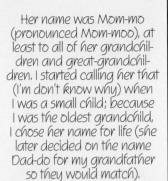

Her name was Mom-mo (pronounced Mom-moo), at least to all of her grandchildren and great-grandchildren. I started calling her that (I'm don't know why) when I was a small child; because I was the oldest grandchild, I chose her name for life (she later decided on the name Dad-do for my grandfather so they would match).

She was my maternal grandmother, and she was in no means an ordinary grandmother. There was not much she couldn't do. She sewed and did needlework like an expert, she cooked (the BEST fried chicken on earth and also some semi-gourmet food), she painted, and she even published two books of poetry when she was in her seventies. Mom-mo was very open-minded for her time and was always non-judgmental.

During college and into my adult years, we didn't make very many long-distance telephone calls, so Mom-mo and I wrote long letters to each other. I have saved so many of them; most are words of encouragement along with her favorite recipe of the moment. To this day I have portions of letters with recipes taped to my recipe notebook. When I turn to a page with a Mom-mo recipe, I'm always reminded of what gorgeous handwriting she had and how much I miss her.

White Almond-Pecan Cake

Anyone who has ever eaten lunch at A la Carte knows that it is bustling from 11 a.m. to 2 p.m. The restaurant sometimes resembles a sort of clubhouse, with the same folks congregating several times a week. Some of our regulars claim a favorite table or a favorite room. And we usually know what they're going to order before they even sit down. Some bring us little gifts when they go on vacation, or tell us about a fabulous restaurant that we must try.

I will never forget one day, one of our loyal customers came in and told me she had something she wanted me to share with everyone at A la Carte. She had brought us a cake she'd purchased while out of town. She wanted us to know how much her family appreciated us! It's moments like this that make me so thankful I live in such a friendly town.

INGREDIENTS FOR CAKE

1	cup butter
1	cup water
2	cups all-purpose flour
1	teaspoon baking soda
1	teaspoon salt
2	cups sugar
2	large eggs, lightly beaten
½	cup sour cream
1	teaspoon almond extract
	Almond Icing

DIRECTIONS FOR CAKE

- Bring butter and 1 cup water to a boil in a large saucepan. Remove from heat.

- Add flour and next 6 ingredients to mixture, stirring well.

- Pour batter into a greased 9 x 13 x 2-inch pan.

- Bake at 375 degrees for 20 minutes. Let cool slightly in pan on a wire rack.

- Spread warm cake with Almond Icing.

INGREDIENTS FOR ALMOND ICING

½	cup butter
¼	cup milk
4½	cups sifted powdered sugar
½	teaspoon almond extract
1	cup chopped pecans

DIRECTIONS FOR ALMOND ICING

- Bring butter and milk to a boil in a saucepan. Remove from heat.

- Gradually add powdered sugar and almond extract, stirring well; stir in pecans.

Serves 16

Jan's Classic Louisiana Pound Cake

INGREDIENTS

2½	cups sugar
1½	cups shortening
4	large eggs
3½	cups cake flour
½	teaspoon baking soda
1	tablespoon warm water
1	teaspoon vanilla extract
1	cup buttermilk

DIRECTIONS

- Beat sugar and shortening at medium speed with an electric mixer until light and fluffy.

- Add eggs to mixture, 1 at a time, beating well after each addition.

- Gradually add flour, stirring with a wooden spoon until blended.

- Combine baking soda and 1 tablespoon warm water, stirring to dissolve. Add baking soda mixture, vanilla, and buttermilk to flour mixture, beating well.

- Pour batter into a greased and floured 10-inch tube pan.

- Bake at 325 degrees for 1 hour or until done.

- Let cake cool in pan on a wire rack 10 to 15 minutes; remove cake from pan and cool completely on wire rack.

Yields 1 (10 inch) cake

There is no such thing as expecting too much.
—Susan Cheever

Everyone loves a good pound cake, and this is my favorite. It is moist and dense and bakes up really tall. My friend Jan has been making this cake for years. She makes one almost every other week and doesn't even look at the recipe. Her cakes always turn out perfectly. I asked her how she can make this all the time and not eat most of it herself. She says she can't restrain herself when it comes to this cake. You'd never think it, though; she NEVER gains weight!

Nettie's Chocolate Fudge Sheet Cake

I have many fond memories of growing up in Trumann, Arkansas, in the 1960s. We lived on Main Street in a house that had a green wooden porch swing. During the summers I practically lived on that swing, reading Nancy Drew books and watching the cars go by. My great-grandmother (Great) lived next door. I always went over to her house when I needed a break from reading. We would eat pimiento cheese sandwiches and drink cokes out of little glass bottles on her sun porch.

Across the street from us lived Nettie Kinman, who was a great cook. Nettie could cook anything, but was known especially for her cakes. She gave this recipe to my mother, and it was the only chocolate cake my brother or I ever asked Mama to make. We now use it for catering at A la Carte, and it is still a favorite.

INGREDIENTS FOR CAKE

2	cups sugar
2	cups all-purpose flour
½	teaspoon salt
1	cup water
½	cup vegetable oil
½	cup butter
3	tablespoons unsweetened cocoa
½	cup buttermilk
1	teaspoon baking soda
1	teaspoon vanilla extract
2	large eggs, lightly beaten
	Chocolate Icing

DIRECTIONS FOR CAKE

- Combine first 3 ingredients in a large bowl.

- Bring 1 cup water and next 3 ingredients to a boil, stirring constantly, in a saucepan; pour over flour mixture, stirring until blended.

- Beat buttermilk, baking soda, and vanilla at medium speed with an electric mixer until creamy; add eggs, beating well.

- Stir egg mixture into flour mixture.

- Pour batter into a greased and floured 9 x 13 x 2-inch pan.

- Bake at 350 degrees for 20 to 25 minutes. Remove from oven and pour Chocolate Icing over hot cake.

INGREDIENTS FOR CHOCOLATE ICING

½	cup butter
3	tablespoons unsweetened cocoa
6	tablespoons evaporated milk
1	tablespoon vanilla extract
½	cup chopped pecans
1	(1-pound) package powdered sugar, sifted

DIRECTIONS FOR CHOCOLATE ICING

- Cook first 3 ingredients in a saucepan over low heat until butter is melted.
- Gradually stir in vanilla, pecans, and powdered sugar.

Serves 12

Anyone who keeps the ability to
see beauty never grows old.
                                    -Franz Kafka

Garnishing With Chocolate

To melt chocolate for decorating, put finely chopped chocolate or chocolate chips in a small, heavy-duty plastic bag (if the bag is not heavy duty, it could melt). Set the unsealed bag upright in a small bowl and microwave at medium (50% power) until almost melted; let stand 5 minutes until completely melted. Or seal the bag and set in a bowl of very hot water until chocolate is melted (make sure no water gets into the chocolate.). Thoroughly dry the bag with a paper towel before snipping a tiny hole in a corner of the bag. Pipe a decorative design directly onto the dessert, or onto a dessert plate.

Banana Cake with Whipped Cream Frosting

This recipe is from a 1938 cookbook that belonged to my paternal grandmother, Alma Beulah Bellers Walton. Mam-ma was a true cook and also a good businesswoman. Her kitchen wasn't lined with cookbooks. She cooked mostly by instinct or memory. Cornbread, mashed potatoes, pot roast, fresh peas, turnip greens, and good home-made desserts were some of her specialties. She had a garden in her backyard and always canned the best dill pickles in the world from her cucumber harvest. She had to ration those quart Mason jars of pickles because everyone wanted them. When I visited, she would carefully wrap a few jars in newspaper for me to take home, and I would hide them from everyone else so I could savor every last bite.

I still to this day miss her cornbread and her pickles. When she passed away, I was the fortunate one to get her perfectly seasoned black iron skillet that she used to make thousand of batches of cornbread. It's my most treasured piece of cookware.

INGREDIENTS

½   cup butter, softened
1⅓   cups granulated sugar
3   large eggs
4   very ripe bananas, mashed
2½   cups all-purpose flour
1   tablespoon baking soda
      Pinch of salt
⅔   cup buttermilk
½   cup chopped nuts (optional)
2   cups whipping cream
¼   cup powdered sugar

DIRECTIONS

- Preheat oven to 350 degrees.
- Beat butter and granulated sugar at medium speed with an electric mixer until creamy; add eggs and banana, mixing well.
- Combine flour, baking soda, and salt in a separate bowl.
- Add flour mixture to banana mixture alternately with buttermilk, beginning and ending with flour mixture; beat until smooth. Stir in nuts, if desired.
- Pour batter into 2 buttered and floured 8-inch round cake pans.
- Bake at 350 degrees for 30 minutes or until a wooden pick inserted in center comes out clean.
- Let cake layers cool in pans on slightly damp tea towels.
- Beat whipping cream with an electric mixer at medium speed in a separate bowl until frothy; gradually add powdered sugar, beating until stiff. Immediately frost top and sides of cooled cake layers.

Yields 1 (8-inch) layer cake

Super-Simple Chocolate-Amaretto Freeze Cake

INGREDIENTS

3   packages ice-cream sandwiches

½   cup amaretto, divided

16   miniature chocolate-covered toffee candy bars, crushed

1   (12-ounce) container frozen whipped topping, thawed

Garnish: toasted sliced almonds

DIRECTIONS

- Line a 9 x 13 x 2-inch baking dish with ice-cream sandwiches.

- Prick sandwiches with a fork and drizzle ¼ cup amaretto over top; sprinkle evenly with half of crushed candy bars.

- Combine remaining ¼ cup amaretto and whipped topping; spread over ice-cream sandwiches.

- Sprinkle evenly with remaining crushed candy bars and, if desired, toasted almonds. Freeze.

Serves 12

A good cook is like a sorceress
who dispenses happiness.
-Elsa Schiaparelli

Almond-Croissant Bread Pudding

With the current revival of old-fashioned desserts, bread pudding has appeared on many dessert menus. It is good comfort food. This bread pudding is special because of the use of croissants. The original recipe called for French bread cubes, but we substituted croissants. We now wouldn't think of using anything else.

INGREDIENTS

10	medium croissants, sliced horizontally
4	large eggs, lightly beaten
1	cup sugar
2	cups milk
½	teaspoon almond extract
½	teaspoon vanilla extract
	Pinch of salt
½	cup chopped almonds

DIRECTIONS

- Place croissants, cut side up, in a buttered baking dish.

- Whisk together eggs and next 5 ingredients; pour over croissant halves. Press down croissant halves and let stand 10 minutes. Press down again so bread absorbs liquid evenly.

- Sprinkle with chopped almonds.

- Bake at 350 degrees for 30 minutes.

Serves 6

If you do nothing unexpected, nothing unexpected happens.

-Fay Weldon

Easy and Elegant Crème Brûlée

INGREDIENTS

8   egg yolks

½   cup granulated sugar

2   cups whipping cream

1   tablespoon vanilla extract

½   cup dried light brown sugar (see directions)

DIRECTIONS

- Preheat oven to 300 degrees.

- Whisk together egg yolks and granulated sugar until thick and pale and sugar is dissolved. Whisk in whipping cream and vanilla.

- Pour mixture into 6 ramekins or custard cups. Place cups in a large roasting pan.

- Make a water bath by filling pan with warm water halfway up the sides of the cups.

- Bake at 300 degrees for 45 to 50 minutes or until mixture is set around the edges but still loose in the center.

- Remove from oven and let cool in water bath.

- Remove crème brûlée from water bath and chill 2 hours or up to 2 days.

- Spread brown sugar thinly on a baking sheet. Bake at 300 degrees for 5 minutes. Remove from oven and let cool. Transfer sugar to a zip-top plastic bag. Finely crush sugar with a rolling pin.

- Sprinkle 2 teaspoons sugar over each serving.

- Caramelize sugar using a small handheld torch or broil until sugar melts.

Serves 6

> She was a butterscotch sundae of a woman.
> -A. J. Liebling

The only dessert on earth that I cannot resist is crème brûlée. In fact, David and I are getting to be experts in sampling. Every restaurant we visit, from Florida to San Francisco, we have to try their crème brûlée. It's amazing to me how many different ways there are to prepare and serve this dessert. The hands-down best we have ever had was at Café Thirty-A in Seagrove Beach, Florida. It was served in a very shallow dish with fresh fruit; it made the perfect "crack" when we spooned into it.

I make crème brûlée at home for special occasions, so I bought the best gadget for home chefs: a small hand-held kitchen torch (available from Williams-Sonoma, 1-800-541-2233). It has an adjustable flame that melts sugar quickly, so the custard beneath stays cool. Hold it 4 to 5 inches away from the sugar, maintaining a slow, steady motion so the sugar will caramelize evenly.

For a variation, place fresh berries evenly in the bottom of the ramekins before pouring in the custard. Proceed with the recipe as directed.

German Chocolate Parfait

INGREDIENTS

1   cup pecans, chopped

1   cup flaked coconut

1   package German chocolate cake mix

1   (8-ounce) package cream cheese

½   cup butter

1   (16-ounce) package powdered sugar

1   (2.05-ounce) chocolate-coated caramel and creamy nougat candy bar

¾   cup evaporated milk

     Whipped cream or vanilla ice cream

DIRECTIONS

- Sprinkle pecans and coconut in the bottom of a 9 x 13 x 2-inch baking dish coated with vegetable cooking spray.

- Prepare cake mix according to package directions; pour over pecans and coconut.

- Melt cream cheese and butter in a saucepan over low heat; add powdered sugar, stirring until blended. Pour over cake batter.

- Bake at 350 degrees for 45 minutes.

- Melt candy bar and evaporated milk in a small saucepan over medium heat, stirring constantly. Let cool slightly.

- Poke holes in top of cake using a fork; slowly pour chocolate mixture over top. Let stand 30 minutes.

- Serve cake in balloon-style red wineglasses or large martini glasses. Top with whipped cream or vanilla ice cream.

Serves 12

Show me a person who doesn't like French fries and we'll swap lies.

—Joan Lunden

How To Make Chocolate Leaves

Chocolate leaves make an extraordinary garnish and they're surprisingly easy to make. Begin by choosing 6 to 8 non-poisonous, firm leaves (such as camellia) with stems attached; wash and thoroughly dry the leaves. Melt about 2 ounces chocolate. Using a small metal spatula or the back of a dinner teaspoon, thickly spread melted chocolate over lthe edges of the leaves; use your fingertip to remove any excess chocolate from the edges. Place the leaves, chocolate side up, on a waxed paper-lined baking sheet; chill until chocolate is set. Hold leaves up to light to look for bare spots. Patch with additional chocolate, then chill again to set. Remove leaf from chocolate by grasping the stem and pulling the leaf gently away from chocolate. Refrigerate chocolate leaves until ready to set.

Jamaican Charlotte

INGREDIENTS

2   dozen macaroons, crumbled
½   cup rum
1   cup butter
1   cup sugar
6   large eggs, separated
2   (1-ounce) unsweetened chocolate squares, melted
½   teaspoon vanilla extract
½   cup chopped pecans
1   dozen double ladyfingers
¾   cup heavy cream
3   tablespoons sugar

DIRECTIONS

- Combine macaroons and rum; let stand.

- Beat butter and sugar at medium speed with an electric mixer until creamy; fold in lightly beaten egg yolks.

- Add macaroon mixture, melted chocolate, vanilla, and pecans to butter mixture, beating well.

- Beat egg whites with an electric mixer at medium speed in a separate bowl until stiff peaks form; fold into chocolate mixture.

- Line a lightly greased 9-inch springform pan with separated ladyfingers, reserving extra ladyfingers.

- Layer chocolate mixture and remaining ladyfingers in prepared pan. Chill overnight.

- Beat cream and sugar with an electric mixer at medium speed in a separate bowl until stiff peaks form. Remove sides of springform pan and decorate with whipped cream.

Serves 12 to 16

Flops are a part of life's menu, and I've never been a girl to miss out on any of the courses.
                              -Rosalind Russell

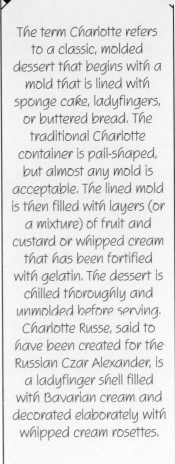

The term Charlotte refers to a classic, molded dessert that begins with a mold that is lined with sponge cake, ladyfingers, or buttered bread. The traditional Charlotte container is pail-shaped, but almost any mold is acceptable. The lined mold is then filled with layers (or a mixture) of fruit and custard or whipped cream that has been fortified with gelatin. The dessert is chilled thoroughly and unmolded before serving. Charlotte Russe, said to have been created for the Russian Czar Alexander, is a ladyfinger shell filled with Bavarian cream and decorated elaborately with whipped cream rosettes.

Chocolate-Praline Torte

This is another quick, easy, and elegant recipe that looks as if you spent a lot of time on it. Rose Miller from Jonesboro, Arkansas, sent it to me. Rose is Nettie's daughter (see Nettie's Chocolate Fudge Sheet Cake, page 138), and she definitely inherited Nettie's love of cooking. Occasionally I will receive a stack of recipes from her in the mail. Great cooks have big hearts.

INGREDIENTS

1½ cups ground pecans
1½ cups vanilla wafer crumbs
1   cup firmly packed light brown sugar
1   cup butter, melted
1   (18.25-ounce) package chocolate cake mix without pudding
    Frozen whipped topping, thawed
    Garnishes: unsweetened chocolate, coarsely grated, and sliced fresh strawberries

DIRECTIONS

- Combine first 4 ingredients, stirring well.

- Sprinkle mixture evenly into 3 lightly greased 8-inch round cake pans.

- Prepare cake mix according to package directions; pour batter evenly into prepared pans.

- Bake at 350 degrees for 15 to 20 minutes.

- Remove cake layers from pans and cool completely on wire racks.

- Spread each layer evenly with whipped topping and stack. Garnish, if desired.

Laughter is the sun that drives winter from the human face.

-Victor Hugo

Easy Tiramisu

INGREDIENTS

1   (7-ounce) package double ladyfingers, separated

½   cup fresh strong brewed coffee (double strength)

¼   cup coffee liqueur

¼   cup sugar, divided

2   teaspoons vanilla extract, divided

1   pound mascarpone cheese

1½   cups heavy cream, whipped

2   teaspoons unsweetened cocoa or ⅓ cup semisweet chocolate, grated

DIRECTIONS

- Arrange half of the ladyfingers in a 9 x 13 x 2-inch baking dish.

- Combine coffee, liqueur, 2 tablespoons sugar, and 1 teaspoon vanilla; brush half of mixture over ladyfingers.

- Beat mascarpone cheese, remaining 2 tablespoons sugar, and remaining 1 teaspoon vanilla at medium speed with an electric mixer 2 minutes. Fold in whipped cream.

- Spoon half of cheese mixture over ladyfingers; top with remaining half of ladyfingers. Brush with remaining coffee mixture. Top with remaining cheese mixture.

- Sift cocoa over top and chill overnight.

Serves 10 to 12

Guard well your spare moments.
They are like uncut diamonds. Discard them
and their value will never be known. Improve
them and they will become the brightest
gems in a useful life.
                        -Ralph Waldo Emerson

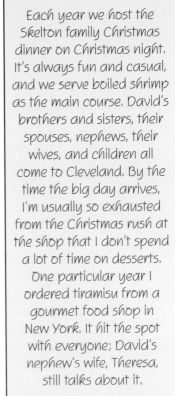

Each year we host the Skelton family Christmas dinner on Christmas night. It's always fun and casual, and we serve boiled shrimp as the main course. David's brothers and sisters, their spouses, nephews, their wives, and children all come to Cleveland. By the time the big day arrives, I'm usually so exhausted from the Christmas rush at the shop that I don't spend a lot of time on desserts. One particular year I ordered tiramisu from a gourmet food shop in New York. It hit the spot with everyone; David's nephew's wife, Theresa, still talks about it.

This recipe tastes just like the one I ordered and is simple to prepare. Maybe this year I'll make it especially for Theresa.

Black Forest Valentine Pie

INGREDIENTS

¾ cup sugar

⅓ cup unsweetened cocoa

2 tablespoons all-purpose flour

¼ cup butter

⅓ cup milk

2 large eggs, lightly beaten

1 (1¼-pound) can cherry pie filling

1 baked 9-inch pastry shell (desired recipe)

1 cup frozen whipped topping, thawed

1 (1-ounce) square unsweetened chocolate, coarsely grated

DIRECTIONS

- Combine first 3 ingredients in a saucepan, stirring well; add butter and milk and bring to a boil, stirring constantly. Remove from heat.

- Add one-fourth of hot mixture to eggs, stirring well. Fold egg mixture into remaining hot mixture.

- Fold one-third of cherry pie filling into chocolate mixture; pour into pastry shell.

- Bake at 350 degrees for 30 to 35 minutes or until center is set but still shiny.

- Let cool and chill 1 hour.

- Combine whipped topping and grated chocolate; spread half of mixture over pie.

- Spread remaining cherry pie filling over pie; top with remaining whipped cream mixture. Chill 1 hour.

Yields 1 (9-inch) pie

You look as pretty as a bag of striped candy.
-Jethro, The Beverly Hillbillies

Key Lime Pie

INGREDIENTS

8   egg yolks

2   (14-ounce) cans sweetened condensed milk

7   ounces Key lime juice

1   (9-inch) deep-dish graham cracker pie crust

DIRECTIONS

- Beat egg yolks at medium speed with an electric mixer until pale.

- Add condensed milk and lime juice to yolks, beating well. Let stand 5 minutes.

- Pour Key lime filling into pie crust. Bake at 350 degrees for 20 minutes or until outside edges are set.

- Let cool on a wire rack. Chill at least 2 hours.

Yields 1 (9-inch) pie

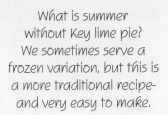

What is summer without Key lime pie? We sometimes serve a frozen variation, but this is a more traditional recipe- and very easy to make.

I always use real Key lime juice (Florribbean brand found at Williams-Sonoma). Key limes are different from regular (Persian) limes in both appearance and taste. Key limes (named after the Florida Keys) are golf ball size and are more yellow than green.

Men are as variable as tea leaves.
Some are gentle, subtle; others are bland like
weak coffee. They can be cloudy and
mysterious, too hot, or too cold. Now and then
you find one who is acidic-a bitter lemon
ruining the flavor of your whole brew. You
have no choice but to throw it out and start
over. And some men, bless their hearts,
are downright sweet.

–Michael Lee West

Chocolate-Strawberry Pie

INGREDIENTS

1¼   cups graham cracker crumbs

3   tablespoons granulated sugar

⅓   cup butter, melted

1   (8-ounce) package cream cheese, softened

¼   cup firmly packed brown sugar

½   teaspoon vanilla extract

3   (1-ounce) bittersweet chocolate squares, melted

1   cup whipping cream

1   cup sliced strawberries

2   (1-ounce) bittersweet chocolate squares

1   teaspoon butter

DIRECTIONS

- Combine first 3 ingredients; press in bottom and up sides of a 9-inch pie plate. Chill.

- Beat cream cheese, brown sugar, and vanilla at medium speed with an electric mixer until fluffy; add melted chocolate, beating well.

- Beat whipping cream at medium speed in a separate bowl until soft peaks form; fold into chocolate mixture.

- Pour chocolate filling into pastry shell. Chill overnight.

- When ready to serve; arrange strawberries on top of pie in overlapping circles.

- Microwave 2 chocolate squares and 1 teaspoon butter in a zip-top plastic bag at HIGH in 10-second intervals, squeezing often, until melted. Snip a small hole in 1 corner of bag and drizzle in a zigzag pattern over strawberries.

Every year for Valentine's Day we sell chocolate-dipped strawberries. We box them to order in attractive containers with big bows. The "chocolate dipping" day is a huge production. Our stainless steel work tables in the kitchen are covered in parchment paper with beautiful red strawberries everywhere. We form an assembly line, and everyone has a job to do. Six of us work nonstop for several hours to keep up with the demand. It is very tiring, but a lot of fun. In honor of all the chocolate-covered strawberry lovers, I came up with this pie recipe that can be enjoyed any day of the year.

You are not old until regrets take the place of dreams.

—John Barrymore

Strawberry Deltalite Pie

INGREDIENTS

1 (3.4-ounce) package strawberry-flavored gelatin

1 cup boiling water

½ cup ginger ale

1 (10-ounce) package frozen sliced strawberries, thawed and drained

1 (16-ounce) container frozen whipped topping, thawed and divided

1 quart fresh strawberries

1 baked 9-inch pastry shell

DIRECTIONS

- Combine gelatin and 1 cup boiling water; add ginger ale, stirring until gelatin is dissolved.

- Stir sliced strawberries into gelatin mixture. Chill until almost set.

- Stir 1 cup whipped topping into gelatin mixture, stirring well.

- Pour filling into pastry shell and decorate with fresh strawberries.

- Chill until firm. Garnish with remaining whipped topping.

Serves 8

If you aren't up to a little magic occasionally,
you shouldn't waste time trying to cook.
—Colette

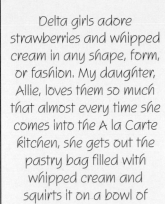

Delta girls adore strawberries and whipped cream in any shape, form, or fashion. My daughter, Allie, loves them so much that almost every time she comes into the A la Carte kitchen, she gets out the pastry bag filled with whipped cream and squirts it on a bowl of fresh strawberries.

Before I became a Delta girl, my mother's strawberry cake is what I requested for birthday celebrations. She would get upset with me because I ate the leftover birthday cake every morning for breakfast until it was gone.

Warm Brownie Pie with Sinful Chocolate Sauce

When we first opened the restaurant, we had only six tables, and our policy was reservations-only because it seemed a "Delta thing" to do! At that time, the only other local eating places were tearooms, and they were reservations-only.

After the first three months, we added six more tables, which were located right in the middle of the gift shop. Customers still tell me how they enjoyed eating and shopping right at their table. Unfortunately, it was hard to sell gifts when the restaurant was full, and we were running out of room. We decided to rent the building across the street and put most of our gifts over there. It sounded like a good idea; more space, and it couldn't be too bad running across the street a few times a day.

At first it was great, but crossing the street 100 times a day eventually got old. Keeping up with inventory in both locations was a nightmare.

(continued)

INGREDIENTS FOR PIE

1	(4-ounce) package sweet chocolate
¼	cup butter
¾	cup sugar
2	large eggs
1	teaspoon vanilla extract
½	cup all-purpose flour
½	cup chopped pecans
	Ice cream
	Chocolate Sauce

DIRECTIONS FOR PIE

- Microwave chocolate and butter in a large bowl at HIGH 2 minutes; stir until chocolate is melted; add sugar, stirring well.

- Add eggs and vanilla to chocolate mixture, stirring well. Add flour and pecans, stirring well.

- Pour pie filling into a greased and floured 9-inch pie plate.

- Bake at 350 degrees for 25 minutes or until a wooden pick inserted in center comes out with crumbs. (Do not overbake.)

- Serve pie warm with ice cream and Chocolate Sauce.

INGREDIENTS FOR CHOCOLATE SAUCE

2	(1-ounce) sweet chocolate squares
⅓	cup water
½	cup sugar
3	tablespoons butter
¼	teaspoon vanilla extract

DIRECTIONS FOR CHOCOLATE SAUCE

- Microwave chocolate and ⅓ cup water at HIGH 1½ minutes; stir until chocolate is melted..

- Add sugar to chocolate and microwave 1 minute; stir well.

- Microwave mixture 2 minutes; stir in butter and vanilla.

Serves 8

One of the goldenest of the golden rules in making up a menu . . . is to pay special attention to the dessert course. . . . Nobody seems able to resist a delicious dessert.
—Wolfgang Puck

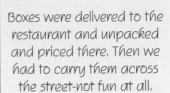

Boxes were delivered to the restaurant and unpacked and priced there. Then we had to carry them across the street-not fun at all.

What to do, what to do . . . we needed more restaurant space, and we all needed to be under one roof. So we moved out of the building across the street, totally gutted and remodeled our storage space in the back of the restaurant, remodeled the kitchen, built a deck overlooking the bayou, and redid the menu all in a month and a half. David drew up the plans and gathered a crew, and they worked daylight till dark to get it ready. We are all under one roof again-gift shop in the front, restaurant in the back-and we can seat 100. We still take reservations, but we also have a room set aside for walk-ins. Now we're all happy.

Neiman-Marcus Brownies

Loyalty is a rare trait these days. That is why we feel so fortunate to have such loyal cooks at A la Carte. Deborah Hines has been with me since day one, and we have worked together so long that we can practically read each other's minds. Deborah started out as a dish-washer, and that job lasted only one day before she was promoted to head cook. When I want to try a new recipe, I go to Deborah and we go over it step by step. She then prepares it for the restaurant.

Deborah's sister Clara came to work three months after we opened. Clara is a perfectionist, and she is the one who makes our fruit, dip, and dessert trays look so beautiful. She assembles all the salads during lunch and also makes the desserts.

Clara and Deborah really didn't want me to give away our secret recipes

(continued)

INGREDIENTS

1   package butter-pecan cake mix
3   large eggs, divided
1   cup butter, melted and divided
1   package powdered sugar
1   (8-ounce) package cream cheese, softened
    Chopped pecans

DIRECTIONS

- Beat cake mix, 1 egg, and ½ cup melted butter at medium speed with an electric mixer until blended.

- Pour batter into a lightly greased 9 x 13 x 2-inch pan.

- Beat remaining 2 eggs, remaining ½ cup melted butter, powdered sugar, and cream cheese at medium speed in a separate bowl until creamy. Pour over batter. Sprinkle with chopped pecans.

- Bake at 350 degrees for 50 to 55 minutes.

- Let cool and cut into squares.

Yields 2 dozen

White Chocolate Pecan Pie

INGREDIENTS

1	(14-ounce) can sweetened condensed milk
⅓	cup white crème de cacao
2	eggs, beaten
4	ounces white chocolate, melted
2	cups chopped pecans
⅓	cup melted butter
3	tablespoons milk
2	teaspoons vanilla
½	teaspoon salt
1	unbaked deep dish pie shell

GARNISH

Pecan halves

DIRECTIONS

- Mix first 3 ingredients in a bowl.

- Stir in next 6 ingredients and pour into pie shell. Arrange pecan halves around outer edge of pie.

- Bake at 425 degrees for 10 to 12 minutes, then reduce oven temperature to 350 degrees. Bake 30 to 35 minutes longer.

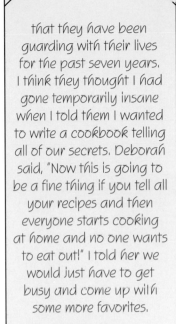

that they have been guarding with their lives for the past seven years. I think they thought I had gone temporarily insane when I told them I wanted to write a cookbook telling all of our secrets. Deborah said, "Now this is going to be a fine thing if you tell all your recipes and then everyone starts cooking at home and no one wants to eat out!" I told her we would just have to get busy and come up with some more favorites.

The Neiman-Marcus Brownie is the most popular dessert bar we make. I bet Clara has made thousands of them.

Billie Ruth's Frozen Peanut Butter Pie

INGREDIENTS

1   (8-ounce) package cream cheese, softened
1½   cups powdered sugar
1½   cups crunchy peanut butter
1   (16-ounce) container whipped topping
2   graham cracker pie crusts
     Grated semi-sweet chocolate

DIRECTIONS

- Beat cream cheese, powdered sugar and peanut butter with an electric mixer. Add whipped topping. Pour into pie crust and sprinkle tops with grated chocolate. Freeze overnight. Serve frozen.

Sweet Potato Pie

INGREDIENTS

1   cup cooked, mashed sweet potatoes
2   cups sugar
3   eggs
1   stick margarine, softened
1   small can evaporated milk
1   teaspoon vanilla
½   teaspoon nutmeg
1   unbaked pie crust

DIRECTIONS

- Mix all ingredients and pour into pie crust. Bake at 350 degrees for 45 to 50 minutes.

Billie Ruth Brewer is one hard-working woman. She has made and delivered mouth-watering sourdough breads to A la Carte every week, and sometimes twice a week for 6 years. Cinnamon rolls, sourdough rolls, loaf bread and jalapeño cheddar breads are eagerly anticipated by our customers.

Not only does she bake at least 100 loaves of bread each week, she drives from Inverness, MS delivering her delicacies to us and to 4 other food establishments in the Delta.

That in itself would make the average person tired, but Billie Ruth also makes pies and casseroles in her "spare" time. Each week she stocks our freezer with her scrumptious pies, places her breads on the counter and is on her way with a smile and a wave. These are 2 of her favorite, easy recipes.

Aileen's 1955 Sour Cream Fudge

INGREDIENTS

2	cups sugar
½	teaspoon salt
1	cup sour cream
2	tablespoons butter
½	cup broken pecans or other nuts

DIRECTIONS

- Cook first 3 ingredients in a saucepan over medium heat, stirring occasionally, until a candy thermometer registers 236 degrees (soft ball stage). Add butter.

- Cool mixture at room temperature, without stirring, until candy thermometer registers 110 degrees (lukewarm).

- Beat with an electric mixer until mixture loses gloss. Stir in pecans.

- Spread mixture into a buttered 8-inch square pan. Let stand until firm. Cut into squares.

Yields 2 dozen pieces

My mother, Aileen, found this recipe in the December 1955 issue of Better Homes and Gardens magazine. That was the same month I was born, and she made it for the first time right before she had me. This has always been my favorite fudge, but I never make it. I still let her make it for me when I eat it.

My mother was a home economics major at the University of Arkansas and Ole Miss in the 1950s. Now that was THE era of homemaking. She was taught not only how to use precision instruments such as candy thermometers and pressure cookers, but also how to make perfect pie crusts from scratch and yeast rolls that would melt in your mouth. They were taught how to keep a spotless home and have well-mannered children. They had sit-down dinners with homemade desserts waiting for their husbands when they came home from work. On top of that, they were supposed to be looking good when they served their men.

My, my, my . . . how times have changed!

Strawberry Orange Trifle

8 cups angel food cake cut into cubes

1 (4¾-ounce) package vanilla pudding mix

3 cups milk

1 tablespoon grated orange peel

3 tablespoons orange juice concentrate

1 (21-ounce) can strawberry pie filling

1 (11-ounce) can mandarin oranges, drained

Whipped cream, fresh whole strawberries for garnish

- Prepare pudding as directed on package using 3 cups milk.
- Remove heat and stir in orange peel. Let cool.
- Line bottom of trifle dish with ⅓ of the cake cubes. Drizzle with 1 tablespoon orange juice concentrate.
- Spoon ⅓ of pudding over top of cake cubes.
- Spread ⅓ of strawberry pie filling over pudding
- Top with ⅓ of mandarin oranges
- Repeat layers 2 more times.
- Cover and refrigerate at least 3 hours.
- Garnish with whipped cream and fresh whole strawberries.

Serves 16

No-Bake Chocolate Kahlua Showstopper

INGREDIENTS

¾ cup Kahlua

½ cup water

24 lady fingers

2 sticks sweet butter, room temperature

1 cup powdered sugar

1 tablespoon almond extract

1⅓ cup ground almonds

½ cup semi-sweet chocolate chips, melted and cooled

2 cups whipping cream

DIRECTION

- Butter a 10-inch springform pan and set it aside.

- Mix together ½ cup Kahlua and ½ cup water. Dip ladyfingers in this and stand them against the sides and bottom of springform pan. Chill.

- Beat together butter and sugar until light and fluffy.

- Add almond extract, ground almonds and melted chocolate; beat until smooth.

- Whip the cream until it is stiff. Add the remaining ¼ cup Kahlua. Fold into the chocolate-butter mixture.

- Place mixture into the springform pan and chill at least 6 hours before serving.

- When you are ready to remove the springform pan, wrap a tea towel that has been soaked in hot water around the pan for a few minutes. Release the spring, use a spatula to remove the bottom plate and place on a cake plate.

This can also be made in a trifle bowl.

Serves 12 to 16

Chocolate Chess Tartlets

INGREDIENTS

½   cup butter

1   (3-ounce) package cream cheese, softened

1   cup all-purpose flour

1   (1-ounce) unsweetened chocolate square

1   tablespoon butter

¾   cup firmly packed brown sugar

1   large egg

1   teaspoon vanilla extract

1   cup chopped walnuts

    Powdered sugar

DIRECTIONS

- Beat butter and cream cheese at medium speed with an electric mixer until creamy; add flour, beating just until blended.

- Wrap dough in plastic wrap and chill 1 hour.

- Shape chilled dough into 36 (1-inch) balls. Flatten each ball and press in bottom and up sides of miniature muffin pan cups.

- Cook chocolate and 1 tablespoon butter in a saucepan over medium-low heat, stirring often, until melted. Remove from heat.

- Add brown sugar, egg, and vanilla, beating with an electric mixer until thickened. Stir in walnuts.

- Spoon 1 teaspoon chocolate filling into each crust.

- Bake at 350 degrees for 20 minutes. Let cool in pans on wire racks 15 minutes.

- Sprinkle tartlets with powdered sugar.

Yields 3 dozen

Deborah's Potato Chip Cookies

This recipe was given to me by Deborah Hines, our head chef, a few weeks after A la Carte opened. To be honest, I thought they sounded horrible when she told me about them.
In order to convince me, she made a batch and I could not believe how delicious they were.
They taste like a crunchy shortbread cookie and get even better a few days after baking.

1   cup sugar

4   sticks butter

1   teaspoon vanilla

3½   cups flour

2   cups crushed potato chips

1   cup chopped pecans, optional

- Preheat oven to 350 degrees.
- Cream together the sugar and butter until light and fluffy.
- Add vanilla and flour, then potato chips and nuts.
- Use ungreased cookie sheets and drop the dough by teaspoonsful onto cookie sheet. You may place them as close as you like because they do not spread.
- Bake 10 to 12 minutes. Remove from cookie sheets and complete cooling on paper towels.

Yields 72 cookies

White Chocolate-Macadamia Cookies

This book would not be complete without telling a little about Miss Daisy. She has helped me do a little bit of everything since I started the gift basket business in my home. She has helped me keep my house presentable, take care of my children, run errands, and even takes care of my cats. She keeps A la Carte clean and has even trained men for the dishwashing position. And when we have the annual "Under the Canopy" sidewalk sale for the gift shop, she is my best salesperson.

One would think with all she does that this is her full-time job. Not on your life-this is only part-time. She has worked full time for 26 years as a nurse's aid at the Bolivar Medical Center. Caring for people is what Daisy does best. She always has others' interests in mind.

Lately, she has been promoting cookbooks that we sell in the gift shop

(continued)

INGREDIENTS

2	cups all-purpose flour
1	teaspoon baking soda
½	teaspoon salt
¾	cup butter, softened
1	cup firmly packed light brown sugar
¾	cup granulated sugar
2	large eggs, at room temperature
1	teaspoon vanilla extract
1	(10-ounce) package white chocolate morsels
1½	cups coarsely chopped macadamia nuts

DIRECTIONS

- Preheat oven to 300 degrees.

- Sift together first 3 ingredients; set aside.

- Beat butter at low speed with an electric mixer 35 to 40 seconds or until creamy; gradually add sugars, beating at medium speed 1 to 2 minutes or until fluffy.

- Add eggs, 1 at a time, beating well after each addition. Add vanilla.

- Gradually stir in flour mixture until blended. Stir in white chocolate morsels and nuts.

- Drop dough by rounded tablespoonfuls onto lightly greased cookie sheets, spacing 1 inch apart. Flatten cookies slightly.

- Bake at 300 degrees for 15 to 20 minutes or until lightly browned around the edges. Let cool and transfer to wire racks.

Yields 3 dozen

Lemon Coffee Shop Cookies

INGREDIENTS

2	cups butter, softened
⅔	cup powdered sugar
2	teaspoons grated lemon rind, divided
½	teaspoon vanilla extract
2	cups all-purpose flour
1½	cups cornstarch
⅓	cup butter, softened
⅓	cup fresh lemon juice
4	cups sifted powdered sugar

DIRECTIONS

- Beat 2 cups butter at medium speed with an electric mixer until creamy; add powdered sugar and beat until fluffy.

- Add 1 teaspoon lemon rind and vanilla, beating well. Gradually add flour and cornstarch, beating well.

- Shape dough into 1-inch balls. Place on ungreased cookie sheets.

- Bake at 350 degrees for 15 minutes or until bottoms are lightly browned.

- Combine remaining 1 teaspoon lemon rind, ⅓ cup butter, lemon juice, and 4 cups powdered sugar, stirring well.

- Remove cookies to wire racks to cool. Spread with lemon frosting.

Yields 6 dozen

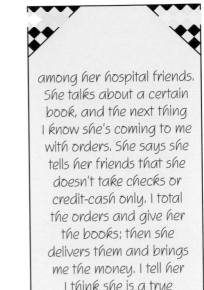

among her hospital friends. She talks about a certain book, and the next thing I know she's coming to me with orders. She says she tells her friends that she doesn't take checks or credit-cash only. I total the orders and give her the books; then she delivers them and brings me the money. I tell her I think she is a true salesperson at heart.

Orange Marmalade Cookies

INGREDIENTS FOR COOKIES

½	cup butter
1	cup sugar
2	eggs, well beaten
3	cups sifted flour
½	teaspoon baking soda
½	teaspoon salt
1	cup thick orange marmalade

INGREDIENTS FOR ICING

¼	cup orange juice
1	teaspoon lemon juice
2	teaspoons grated orange peel
1	teaspoon grated lemon peel
3	tablespoons soft butter
3	cups confectioners' sugar
⅛	teaspoon salt

DIRECTIONS FOR COOKIES

- Cream butter. Add sugar and continue beating until light and fluffy.

- Mix in eggs. Beat in flour, soda and salt.

- Add marmalade and blend.

- Drop by teaspoonsful 1 inch apart on a well-buttered cookie sheet.

- Bake at 350 degrees 10 to 12 minutes. Let cool and frost.

DIRECTIONS FOR ICING

- Mix juices and peels. Cream butter and sugar. Mix all together and blend. Add salt and mix until spreading consistency.

Yields 3 dozen

Trade Secrets

How many appetizers to make per person for a dinner or cocktail party?

- I have researched hundreds of cookbooks, trade magazines and cooking publications and have found the following formula to be the most consistent among professionals.

  COCKTAIL PARTY: 12 APPETIZERS PER PERSON

  DINNER PARTY: 6 APPETIZERS PER PERSON

- This is a fairly standard formula used among caterers to figure out how many appetizers are needed from each recipe.

  12 pieces per person times the number of people divided by the number of different appetizers. (When they are being served before a full dinner, halve the totals.)

  If the guest list has fewer than 45 people, plan on using roughly 6 different appetizers; for more than 45 guests, 8 types. The rule of thumb for smaller gatherings is that 3 types are suitable for 8 to 10 guests; 4 or 5 for 14 to 16 people.

- Having an equal number of hot and cold foods is also helpful so that while one appetizer is heating in the oven, a cold one can be circulating.

Home-Fried Tortilla Chips

INGREDIENTS

24   corn tortillas
2   quarts sunflower or safflower oil
    Salt to taste

DIRECTIONS

- Stack tortillas into piles of 6; with a sharp knife, cut each stack into 6 to 8 equal wedges. Spread the wedges onto paper towels.

- When the temperature registers between 375 and 400 degrees on a deep-fat thermometer, add a handful of tortilla wedges into an electric deep fryer. Fry for 1 minute, stirring once or twice. Do not crowd the fryer, and fry the chips only until they're crisp but not too dark. Transfer chips with a slotted spoon to paper towels, and season with salt. Continue frying other wedges.

Yields 12 to 14 dozen chips

Mayonnaise

- A wide selection of mayonnaise can be found in markets today—from real to imitation, and in styles ranging from nonfat to low-fat to regular. At A la Carte, we use a heavy duty commercial type mayonnaise we get from a food supplier which is similar to HELLMAN'S. If you don't have the time to make homemade mayonnaise, this is the brand we suggest.

- A trade secret to give a fresh taste to commercial mayonnaise is to stir in 1 to 2 teaspoons of good wine vinegar, lemon juice or lime juice.

- You may also personalize mayonnaise by stirring in herbs or other flavorings. Add minced, fresh herbs like basil, dill or cilantro; finely grated lemon zest; or horseradish; or minced sun-dried tomatoes; or curry or chili powder. Whatever you like.

Homemade Mayonnaise

INGREDIENTS

- 12 egg yolks
- 1 whole egg
- 1 tablespoon Dijon mustard
- Pinch of salt
- Freshly ground black pepper, to taste
- 2 to 4 tablespoons fresh lemon juice
- 2 cups corn, vegetable or olive oil (extra virgin olive oil can overpower the flavor of homemade mayonnaise, so it is best to use either a mild olive oil, or half extra-virgin and half vegetable oil.)

DIRECTIONS

- Combine the egg yolks, whole egg, mustard, salt, pepper and 2 tablespoons of the lemon juice in a food processor; process for 1 minute.

- With the motor running, gradually add the oil through the feed tube in a slow, steady stream. When the mayonnaise is thoroughly blended, turn the processor off and scrape down the sides of the bowl. Taste and correct the seasonings. If you are using vegetable oil, you will probably need the remaining 2 tablespoons lemon juice.

- Cover and refrigerate. Let it return to room temperature before stirring and using.

Olive Salad for Muffaletta Sandwich or A la Carte Italian Pasta Salad

At A la Carte, we purchase our olive salad we use for muffaletta sandwiches from our food supplier. However, this is a homemade version that is very similar.

INGREDIENTS

¾   cup black calamata olives, pitted and coarsely chopped
¾   cup green olives, coarsely chopped
1   clove garlic, mashed
1-2   tablespoons small capers
¼   cup finely chopped red onion
¼   cup finely chopped fresh parsley
2   tablespoons diced red pimento peppers
½   teaspoon oregano
     Several dashes of coarsely ground black pepper
2   tablespoons extra virgin olive oil
1   tablespoon lemon juice

DIRECTIONS

- Mix all the ingredients together in a small bowl one day before you want to serve it so the flavors will blend.

Pesto

At A la Carte, we use a commercial pesto sauce available at most grocery stores. However, if you are industrious, you might like making your own. This is an easy version.

HOMEMADE PESTO

4	cloves garlic, minced
2	cups fresh basil leaves, rinsed and dried
⅓	cup extra virgin olive oil
½	teaspoon salt
½	teaspoon black pepper

DIRECTIONS

- Place the garlic and basil in the bowl of a food processor. With the motor running, slowly drizzle in the oil through the feed tube, and process until the basil is puréed.

- Transfer pesto to a bowl and add the salt and pepper.

Yields ¾ cup

If you grow your own basil in the summer, it can be frozen for use all year long. Finely chop cleaned basil leaves, then combine with enough olive oil to make a paste. Spoon tablespoonsful of the paste into ice cube trays or onto a plastic wrap-lined baking sheet and freeze until solid. Then transfer to a plastic bag and use as needed to flavor sauces, soups, salad dressings, etc.

How to Boil Shrimp

INGREDIENTS

5	pounds medium-size shrimp, rinsed
2	boxes Zatarain crawfish, shrimp and crab boil seasoning bags
½-1	cup salt
	Juice of 2-3 large lemons
2	teaspoons cayenne pepper
4-6	quarts water

DIRECTIONS

- Bring water, salt, lemon juice, cayenne pepper and seasoning bags to boil in a very large stock pot. Bring to a vigorous boil and let boil for 5 minutes. Add shrimp (boiling will stop or slow down). Set timer for 5 minutes. When timer goes off, remove stock pot from burner; place top on stock pot. Set timer for 3 to 5 minutes. Check shrimp after a few minutes, because when the shrimp sink to the bottom of the pot, they need to be drained immediately. Have a large colander ready in the sink. Drain shrimp and immediately pour ice over the top of them in the colander. This stops them from cooking any further. Allow them to drain thoroughly.

SHRIMP SIZES

- How many shrimp you get per pound depends on the size. Though it varies from market to market, the average number per pound is as follows:

Colossal	10 or fewer
Jumbo	11 to 15
Ex. Large	16 to 20
Large	21 to 30
Medium	31 to 35
Small	36 to 45
Miniature	60 to 100

How to Poach Chicken Breasts

- Start by filling a large stock pot with enough water to cover the chicken breasts. A few splashes of white wine may be added if desired. Add several onion slices, celery leaves and season with salt and pepper. Add chicken breasts. Bring the pot to a full boil, and then turn it off, letting the heat of the liquid finish the cooking process.

- When everything has cooled, remove chicken breasts with a slotted spoon. The poaching liquid can be strained and used for stock in soup recipes (this can be frozen).

Jazzed-Up Purchased Barbecue Sauce

Bottled barbecue sauce can become "homemade" in just a few minutes by customizing it with any of the following additions:

- lemon, orange or lime juice and/or zest
- chopped fresh chile peppers, dried red pepper flakes, cayenne or Tabasco sauce
- maple syrup, honey, molasses or brown sugar
- chopped fresh herbs such as basil, cilantro, oregano or parsley
- minced fresh ginger root
- horseradish or spicy brown mustard
- minced, fresh tomatoes
- minced garlic, green pepper or onion
- sherry or full-bodied beer
- worcestershire or soy sauce
- sesame or olive oil
- ground peanuts

Hints for Perfect Cakes

- Butter your cake pans with butter or spray them with a light coating of nonstick spray. Sprinkle flour into each pan and shake it until it is coated. Tap out excess flour.

- Fill your pans no more than two-thirds full of batter and make sure the batter is spread all the way into the sides and corners of the baking pan.

- When the cake is baked it should shrink slightly from the sides of the pan. Invest in a small cake tester (or use a clean toothpick) to accurately check to see if your cake is thoroughly baked. Insert the tester into the center of the cake and it will come out clean when the cake is done.

- The best way to keep a cake from sinking or falling is to place the hot cake pan directly onto a tea towel that has been soaked in water and wrung out. The cake pan will make a hissing sound, but the cake will cool perfectly and come out almost as high as it was when it was taken out of the oven. Allow cakes to cool completely before removing them from cake pans.

- For layer cakes, freeze the cake layers for at least one hour before frosting them. Most cake layers can be covered with foil or clear plastic wrap and stored for weeks before using them.

- Place one layer rounded side down on the cake platter so that the flat side of the cake is on the top. If the bottom of the cake is a little too dark, scrape away that part using a potato peeler. Brush off any cake crumbs so that they don't get mixed into the frosting.

- Spread frosting on top of the layer almost to the edge. Place the second layer flat side down on top of the bottom layer with the rounded side up. Frost the sides of the cake.

- Cover the top of the cake with frosting, making sure that the top frosting meets the side frosting.

- Be creative with the final touches. Use a pastry tube to decorate the top and bottom edges of the cake and garnish with fresh fruit, fresh flowers, nuts, or whatever looks good.

Index

A la Carte Alley

111 South Court Street
Cleveland, MS 38732

Order Phone: (662) 843-1955
Fax: (662) 843-6512
Email: alacarte@capital2.com

Please send me _____ copy(ies) of **Absolutely A la Carte**

$21.95 per copy _____

$ 3.00 postage _____

Mississippi residents only: $ 1.53 sales tax _____

TOTAL _____

Makes check payable to: **A la Carte Alley**

Name _____

Address _____

City _____ State _____ Zip _____

Please charge to my VISA _____ or MASTERCARD _____
DISCOVER _____ AMEX _____

Card number _____

Expiration date _____

Cardholder's signature _____

From:
A la Carte Alley
111 South Court Street
Cleveland, MS 38732

MAILING LABEL - PLEASE PRINT

Name

Address

City & State

Zip Code

A la Carte Alley

111 South Court Street
Cleveland, MS 38732

Order Phone: (662) 843-1955
Fax: (662) 843-6512
Email: alacarte@capital2.com

Please send me _____ copy(ies) of **Absolutely A la Carte**

$21.95 per copy _____

$ 3.00 postage _____

Mississippi residents only: $ 1.53 sales tax _____

TOTAL _____

Makes check payable to: **A la Carte Alley**

Name _____

Address _____

City _____ State _____ Zip _____

Please charge to my VISA _____ or MASTERCARD _____
DISCOVER _____ AMEX _____

Card number _____

Expiration date _____

Cardholder's signature _____

From:
A la Carte Alley
111 South Court Street
Cleveland, MS 38732

MAILING LABEL - PLEASE PRINT

Name

Address

City & State

Zip Code